HOW TO
PLAY PIANO

Books in the HOW TO PLAY Series

How to Play Bass Guitar
BY LAURENCE CANTY

How to Play Guitar
BY ROGER EVANS

How to Play Drums
BY JAMES BLADES AND JOHNNY DEAN

How to Play the Flute
BY HOWARD HARRISON

How to Play Keyboards
BY ROGER EVANS

How to Play Piano
BY ROGER EVANS

HOW TO PLAY PIANO

Everything You Need to Know to Play the Piano

Roger Evans

St. Martin's Griffin
New York

HOW TO PLAY PIANO. Copyright © 1981 by Roger Evans. All rights reserved. Printed in the United States of America. For information, address St. Martin's Press, 175 Fifth Avenue, New York, N.Y. 10010.

www.stmartins.com

Library of Congress Cataloging-in-Publication Data

Evans, Roger.
How to play piano.
ISBN 0-312-28708-9
1. Piano—Instruction and study. I. Title.

MT220.E88
786.3'041   81-5822

D 40 39 38

Contents

This book is dedicated to my father, Norman L. Evans,
who introduced me to the pleasure of making my own music

HOW TO
PLAY PIANO

Introduction

This new book is for everyone who would like to play the piano. It is for the absolute beginner, and for those who once started to play and would like to take up the piano again.

Everything you need to know to start playing the piano is explained here in easy-to-understand stages, so you can begin to learn how to play the music of your choice: Classical, Pop, Rock, Blues, Jazz and other styles. You need have no previous knowledge of music or the piano to start playing immediately and entertain yourself by making your own music.

How quickly you learn depends entirely on you. With this book, you can learn at your own speed, or you can use it with piano lessons. There are no boring exercises, instead there are interesting pieces of music to play — so learning is fun right from the beginning.

Read a few pages at a time and make sure you understand everything before going on. If necessary, read the same page several times until you know exactly what is meant. Do not skip any pages or jump back and forth, or you may miss something important.

You will find the piano an uncomplicated instrument to play. It will give you a lot of enjoyment as long as you take the time to learn to do everything correctly. In this way you will avoid getting into bad habits, which may limit your playing later on. On the piano, you will find the right way to play is not only the best, but also the easiest in the long run.

This book is the result of many years playing and teaching music. I hope the benefit of my experience will introduce you to a great deal of pleasure playing the piano.

Roger Evans

About the Piano

Every year, more and more people discover how much fun it is to make their own music at home, and every year more and more people start to play the piano. This is not really surprising, because the piano is an enjoyable instrument to play, and it produces a very pleasant sound.

The piano is also a very versatile instrument. It can be used to play the melody of a tune, or the melody and backing together, or it can provide a pleasing accompaniment for other instruments and for singing. It can be played on its own, within a group or band, or in an orchestra.

The piano has a larger range of notes than most of the instruments in an orchestra and is suitable for almost every different style of music. This makes it excellent for learning music, and for composing and arranging.

Beginners of all ages can make pleasant sounding music almost immediately on the piano, because the notes are easy to find and play.

Above all, it is a satisfying and entertaining instrument — both beginners and experienced players will find an almost limitless variety of music which can be played on the piano.

DIFFERENT TYPES OF PIANOS

There are basically two different types of pianos — grand pianos and upright pianos.

Grand pianos have their strings arranged horizontally, rather like a harp lying on its side. The very first pianos were made in this way, although they did not look much like the modern grand piano.

Upright pianos, as their name suggests, have their strings and most of their working parts arranged vertically.

Both types of piano come in various shapes and sizes, but they are all basically similar to play. The main parts of the piano which you can see from the outside are named on the facing page.

DIFFERENT TYPES OF PIANOS

LID_____

LID PROP_____

MUSIC RACK_____

FALL (Covers Keys)_____

KEYBOARD_____

PIANO STOOL
OR BENCH_____

PEDALS_____

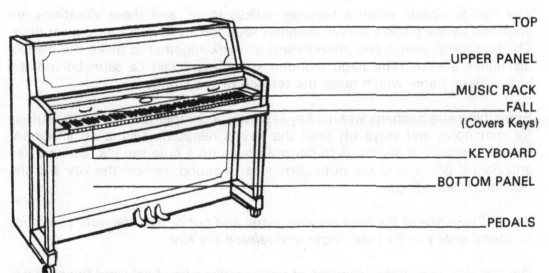

GRAND PIANO

TOP

UPPER PANEL

MUSIC RACK

FALL
(Covers Keys)

KEYBOARD

BOTTOM PANEL

PEDALS

UPRIGHT PIANO

9

How a piano works

You will get the best out of your piano if you know a little about the way it works.*

All the notes on the piano are set out in a very simple way. The notes sound higher and higher as you move to the right of the keyboard, and lower and lower as you move to the left. *With one finger, try pushing down different white and black keys on your piano, one after the other, and compare their different sounds.* Hear how each note sounds higher than the note before as you move to the right, and lower than the note before as you move to the left.

Open up your piano and see what happens when you play a note. (You can see most of the working parts if you open the lid of a grand piano, or open the top and upper panel of an upright piano. Be careful not to touch the inside parts of the piano or the delicate mechanism could be damaged.)

Now play a few notes again, and watch what happens inside the piano. Notice how each note is made when a felt-covered hammer strikes some of the strings. In fact, each note has its own hammer and strings. There are usually three strings for each of the higher sounding 'treble' notes, and two thicker copper-wound strings for each of the lower 'bass' notes. A few of the very lower notes may have only *one* very thick wire-wrapped string each.

The strings vibrate when a hammer strikes them, and these vibrations are amplified by the piano's curved wooden soundboard to give a loud clear note. The hammers, strings and soundboard all work together to make the piano's distinctive sound. (The large wooden soundboard can be seen behind the heavy metal frame which takes the tension of the strings.)

Something else happens when a key is struck: a damper felt lifts off the strings for that note, and stays off until the key is released. This is an important feature, because it allows us to control how long a note sounds. Strike a key and hold it down, and the note continues to sound; release the key and the note stops sounding.

Try it. Strike one of the keys on your piano and notice how the note continues to sound until you lift your finger and release the key.

We can also control the loudness of notes: strike a key firmly and the note will be loud, strike gently and the note will be soft.

Try striking a key firmly and then gently and compare the loud and soft sounding notes which you hear.

*Read this chapter and the one which follows if you are buying a piano, even though you cannot follow all the instructions.

The pedals of the piano also affect its sound:

THE RIGHT (SUSTAINING) PEDAL. This pedal sustains notes, so that they last longer than they normally would. Contrary to popular belief it does not make notes sound louder.

When the right pedal is pressed down, the damper felts are lifted off *all* the strings, so that each note played continues to sound after its key is released.

This pedal can be very helpful to the experienced player. However, it will cause piano playing to sound jumbled if used incorrectly. For this reason, the beginner should not use the right (sustaining) pedal until other aspects of playing have been learned.

THE LEFT (SOFT) PEDAL. This pedal makes the piano sound softer.

When the left pedal is pressed down on an upright piano, the hammers move closer to the strings, so that they strike the strings with less force and produce less sound. On grand pianos, the soft pedal moves the entire keyboard slightly to the right, so each hammer strikes fewer strings for each note, giving a softer, thinner sound.

The soft pedal is used for special effects in some music. It can also be helpful if you wish to play without disturbing other people.

THE MIDDLE PEDAL. This may produce one of several different effects:

On some pianos, it is a 'sostenuto' pedal which enables selected notes to be sustained while other notes are played normally. This feature would normally only be used by very accomplished pianists.

On other pianos, the middle pedal may be an extra-soft pedal, or it may activate a mechanism which gives the piano a 'jangling' sound.

Do not be concerned if your piano does not have a middle pedal — it is not needed for most piano playing.

Try playing different notes with each of the pedals pressed down in turn, so that you can watch what happens inside the piano and hear the different sounds each pedal gives. Notice that the effect of each pedal ceases when you take your foot off.

REMEMBER to close your piano when you have finished watching the different parts work, so that no damage is caused to the mechanism.

Checking your piano

Check your piano before you play it for the first time. This is important, because if anything is wrong, the piano may be difficult to play or sound unpleasant — both of which could take the fun out of learning to make your own music.

First, find out when the piano was last tuned. Your piano will need to be tuned as soon as possible, unless it has been tuned in the last six months. It will also need tuning if it has been moved from one house to another, or up or down stairs since it was last tuned.

Next, check that every note plays properly. Do this by striking each key on the piano, one at a time. Make sure that every key pushes down equally easily, and comes back smoothly and silently to the level of the other keys when you take your finger off. Every note should sound as loudly and clearly as the note next to it. If any notes are weaker than the others or sound out of tune, or if any of the keys are noisy or stiff, something is wrong and the piano needs attention.

Finally, press down each of the pedals to make sure they work smoothly and silently. Even though you will probably not need them for a while, it is as well to have them adjusted, if necessary, when other work is done or when the piano is tuned.

What do you do if the piano needs tuning or has any faulty notes?
If the piano is your own instrument, you need to find a good piano tuner-technician, if you do not already know one. (Some hints on finding a piano tuner-technician are given on page 13.)

If the piano belongs to someone else and seems to have something wrong with it, tell the owner that it appears to need tuning or repairing.

In either case, the piano should be tuned or repaired as soon as possible.

Should you play the piano before it is tuned or repaired?
If all of the keys in the middle of the keyboard work properly, and the notes they make sound reasonably good, you can start to play while you wait for the piano to be tuned or repaired.

However, if any of the middle keys do not work properly, or if their notes sound bad, be patient and wait until the piano has been fixed before you start playing. It would be a pity if faulty keys or a poor sound make piano playing less enjoyable for you.

Having your piano tuned

Your piano should be tuned at least twice a year (three times a year is better) even if it has not been played at all.

A regularly tuned piano is enjoyable to play, for the beginner as well as the expert. Even simple music sounds good on a well-tuned piano, but if the piano is out of tune, everything played on it will sound unpleasant.

Tuning does more than make the piano sound pleasant, it also adjusts the tension of the strings. This is very important, because the strings exert an enormous force which can distort or even crack the soundboard and other parts, if the piano is not tuned regularly and correctly.

The strings are at the correct tension when the piano is tuned to 'concert pitch', which is the standard for tuning all musical instruments. Have your piano tuned to 'concert pitch', and you will avoid a major cause of damage, the piano will sound better, and it will be tuned correctly for playing with other instruments.

FINDING A GOOD PIANO TUNER
The very best person to look after your piano is a tuner-technician who not only tunes pianos, but also adjusts and repairs them.

The best way to find one of these skilled individuals is on the recommendation of someone who plays the piano seriously. Ask a friend who plays the piano, or see if the music department of a local school or college, a local music society or local piano shop can recommend someone they deal with. Otherwise, look for piano tuner-technicians in the 'Yellow Pages' of the telephone directory, or in advertisements in music magazines or newspapers.

Make an appointment with the tuner-technician and explain what you think needs to be done. Ask for the piano to be tuned to 'concert pitch', even though this may cost extra the first time it is done. Allow at least two hours for the piano to be tuned and pick a time when your home will be quiet, so that the tuner can work without being distracted.

Remove anything which is on top of the piano before the tuner comes, so nothing gets in the way of the work.

If your tuner-technician suggests that other work is required, you will probably be well advised to have it done. However, if the piano is very old or has been badly treated, you may be better off considering buying another instrument. Ask for your tuner's advice and get an estimate of the cost of any work.

Stay with the same tuner-technician when you find a good one and make regular appointments so your piano will be well cared for.

Taking care of your piano

Follow the hints given here and your piano should stay in the best possible condition and be a joy to play for many years.

If something is wrong with the piano, have it corrected immediately.
Have any faulty keys, poor-sounding notes or faulty pedals adjusted immediately by a qualified tuner-technician. Parts which go out of adjustment will only get worse if left uncorrected and may cause extra wear to themselves or other parts. Having parts adjusted when a problem first occurs is far cheaper than replacing worn parts later on.

Have the piano tuned at least twice a year to 'concert pitch'.
As explained earlier, the piano should be tuned to the correct pitch at least twice a year to avoid damage. Regular tuning will also help the strings to last longer and allow the piano to sound at its best.

It is not a good idea to try and save money by having the piano tuned less frequently — any money spent on tuning or repairs and adjustments will be more than repaid by the longer life you can expect for your piano if it is given regular attention.

Do not try to tune, repair or clean the inside of your piano yourself.
There are thousands of different parts in a piano, many of which need expert adjustment to work properly. Expensive damage to the delicate mechanism can easily be caused by accident, so it is best to leave all work on the inside mechanism to your tuner-technician. However, do not expect everything to be adjusted or cleaned during a regular tuning visit because it would take too long. If extra work needs to be done, call your tuner in advance and make a special appointment.

Clean the piano case and keyboard yourself.
You can clean all the black and white keys by wiping them with a soft cloth, slightly dampened with methylated spirit. When they are dry, polish the keys with a soft dry cloth.

Clean the outside case (furniture) of the piano with a wax furniture polish — unless the piano manufacturer recommends otherwise. However, do not use a polish which contains silicones as they leave a permanent coating which cannot be removed if the piano needs refinishing. Keep polish away from the keys and wash your hands before playing.

Keep the piano closed when it is not being played.
Play with the top of the piano open so the piano will sound its best, but close the top and fall when you are not playing to stop dust or anything else getting inside and damaging the mechanism. If there are small children in the home, make sure they do not have the opportunity to open up the piano — little fingers can do a surprising amount of damage to musical instruments.

Do not put heavy items on top of the piano or they may spoil the finish.
Never place a plant or a vase containing water on top of a piano — if water or any other liquid gets inside the piano it could cause serious damage.

Repairs to the piano case.
Call in a piano repairer, *not* a regular furniture repairer, if any work needs to be done to the outside case of the piano to avoid the inside mechanism being damaged during any refinishing.

You may need a piano dehumidifier.
Extreme humidity and rapid changes of temperature can damage a piano and make it go out of tune quickly. If you live in an area with high humidity, ask your tuner if you need a dehumidifier to avoid these problems. Never place your piano close to a radiator as too much dryness is also harmful.

Keep moths and beetles out of your piano.
Pianos can be damaged by clothes moths and various beetles, so put one or two old-fashioned moth balls on a paper plate in the bottom of the piano, well away from any moving parts. Most insects and other intruders will then keep out of your piano, particularly if you keep it completely closed when you are not playing it.

Talk to your tuner-technician about your piano.
If your tuner-technician knows you are taking a more than normal interest in your piano, he or she will probably take special care of it and watch for anything which requires attention before it becomes serious. Do not hesitate to ask for advice — most people who work with musical instruments are pleased to explain how an instrument works, or how it could be better cared for, as long as you do not take too much of their time.

Other hints to help you take care of your piano are given on page 16. Also read 'Buying a piano' which follows, even if you already have a piano, to learn more about your instrument.

The best place for your piano

Ideally, your piano should be in a constant temperature of 70°F (21°C) with 40% humidity, in a well-soundproofed room so you can play loudly whenever you like without anyone hearing. Unfortunately, very few of us have such a room, but it is usually possible to find somewhere suitable for a piano in most homes, if you follow the hints given here:

If possible, your piano should be in a room where you can be on your own when you want to play. Everyone needs to be able to practise and try out new music in private without having an audience listening to any mistakes. If it is not possible to have your piano in a separate room, try to plan times for playing when no one else will be around to listen.

You may need to consider your family or neighbours, because the sound of a piano carries through walls and floors. Avoid putting your piano near the wall of someone else's lounge or bedroom and do not play late at night to avoid disturbing others. (If necessary, the sound of a piano can be reduced by standing the instrument on a thick carpet and by hanging a thick rug on the wall behind an upright piano. You can also make the piano quieter by using the soft pedal, but this is not satisfactory all the time.)

Sudden changes of temperature or humidity can damage a piano and sour its tuning, so you should choose a place for your piano which is away from radiators, air-conditioning or heating outlets. Also avoid putting the piano by a window or door where there is a draught, or where the sun could shine on it and damage the outside finish or inside mechanism. Leaving a gap of about 6in. (15cm) between the back of an upright piano and a wall to allow air to circulate freely.

MOVING A PIANO
Never try to move a piano on your own, because you could seriously injure yourself or damage the piano.

Pianos are very heavy. Use professional piano movers to move a piano up or down stairs, or from one building to another. Ask friends to help you push it, if you want your piano in another room on the same floor. Grand pianos need very careful handling to avoid their legs collapsing — make sure the piano legs are secure *before* and *after* a grand is moved. (Ask your local piano store to recommend piano movers, if you need them.)

Have the tuning checked one month after the piano is moved up or down stairs or to another building, as the move may put the piano out of tune.

Buying a piano

Buying a piano is a great adventure, particularly if you have never owned one before. A good piano is an investment which should bring you a great deal of pleasure and be your pride and joy for many years.

If you have already started to look at pianos, you will realise there is a very large choice of instruments on the market. There are pianos in many different shapes and sizes, at various prices. There are pianos which look like pianos, and pianos which look like any one of a dozen different styles of furniture with various wooden or painted finishes. A great selection, but how do you decide which is best for you? Before you do anything, read these friendly words of advice to make sure you are buying the right type of piano and getting good value for your money.

SIZE. As a general rule, large pianos are the best pianos because they have sufficient internal space for long strings and large soundboards — both of which are needed to produce a mellow tone and good volume. Your first choice should therefore be the largest piano which will fit into your home.

GRAND PIANOS. If you can find sufficient space in your home, and can afford the purchase price, a grand piano is the best choice.

So, before you consider anything else, measure your home and see if you have room for a grand. You should bear in mind the advice given on page 16 about the best place for a piano, before you finally decide. The usual sizes of grand pianos are given here:

APPROXIMATE SIZES OF GRAND PIANOS

	LENGTH	WIDTH	HEIGHT
Concert Grand	96in. (240cm) or longer		
Medium Grand	72-90in. (180-225cm)	60in. (150cm)	40in. (100cm)
Small Grand	54-66in. (135-170cm)		

The largest grand pianos, concert grands, are the finest pianos made. Most pianists dream of owning one because they are a joy to play and produce the finest tone. However, they are unfortunately too large for most homes.

The next choice should be for a medium grand — most of these are fine instruments, well-suited for use in the home. Third choice should be a small grand piano.

Do not despair if your home is not large enough to take a grand piano — many full-size uprights and studio pianos are as good as small grands.

17

UPRIGHT PIANOS. The overall height of an upright piano is a good guide to the musical quality of the instrument. Note that all upright pianos need approximately the same amount of floor space — about 5' (150cm) by 2' (30cm), except for the narrower 64 note spinet.

APPROXIMATE SIZES OF UPRIGHT PIANOS

	HEIGHT	LENGTH	WIDTH
Full-size	48in. (120cm) or more		
Studio	44-46in. (112-117cm)	60in. (150cm)	24in. (60cm)
Console	40-42in. (100-108cm)		
Spinet	36-38in. (90-96cm)		
64 Note Spinet	36-38in. (90-96cm)	42in. (108cm)	24in. (60cm)

First choice for musical quality should be a full-size upright or a studio piano. Second choice should be a console piano, although here you are compromising musical quality for the sake of price or appearance as a piece of furniture.

Spinet pianos, particularly the narrower 64 note spinets, come last as musical instruments. These pianos are not large enough to allow room for a proper working mechanism, a good size soundboard or sufficiently long strings to ensure a good quality tone or volume. Also, 64 note spinets do not have the full range of eighty-eight notes of a full-size piano.

SHOP AROUND BEFORE YOU BUY. Spend some time shopping around and compare as many different pianos as possible. Even if you do not play at all, you can learn a lot about the different pianos which are available by talking to piano dealers and reading the brochures which makers supply.

Specialist piano stores are the best places to look at pianos. Good piano dealers will understand what you want, give useful advice and help you to compare different pianos without rushing you to make a decision. Look for piano stores in the 'Yellow Pages', or in music magazines or newspapers.

If you can, visit stores on weekdays when the sales people should have more time to spend with you. Go to as many stores as possible to see a wide range of pianos, and try to find dealers who take a pride in the quality of their pianos because they will give the best advice.

Ask to be shown the insides of pianos which interest you, and have the internal features explained, so you will know which piano is best.

PRICE. The advice of piano experts is to buy the very best piano you can afford. A piano is a long-term investment — if you buy a good instrument and take care of it, it should have a useful life of forty or fifty years. Think about this before you decide how much to pay for a piano. All pianos are expensive. However, good pianos are not necessarily very much more expensive than poor pianos, and could turn out cheaper in the long run — because a good piano should last longer and require less attention.

Do not buy the cheapest piano of any type in any range, as quality may have been sacrificed for the sake of price. If you have to choose between two pianos at a similar price, buy the one with the best internal mechanism, instead of the piano which is the fanciest piece of furniture. (The hints which follow explain how to judge the quality of the mechanism.)

If you find you cannot afford a good new piano, you might consider looking for a suitable secondhand instrument (see below). Alternatively, you may be able to rent a piano for your home — some piano stores can arrange this — or learn to play on a piano in a school or hall, provided you can get to play it often enough.

SECONDHAND PIANOS. Good secondhand pianos can sometimes be found at reasonable prices. Used grand pianos, in particular, can be a good 'buy' if you find someone who is moving to a smaller home. However, any used piano must be checked very carefully if you are not to waste your money.

Secondhand pianos are sold by some piano stores, but even here you have to be careful to avoid poor pianos. The best advice is only to consider nearly new pianos or instruments which have recently been *completely* reconditioned by a professional piano repairer.

Do not consider any piano which has been used in a school, church or other public place because it will have had heavy use. Also avoid any piano over twenty years old, unless it has been completely re-built.

If you are thinking of buying a piano privately, you should have it inspected by a professional tuner-technician. The fee for this service is very worthwhile, as it will remove the risk of your paying more than a piano is worth, and stop you buying a poor quality or worn-out piano. A tuner-technician may also know of good second-hand pianos for sale in your area. (See page 13 for how to find a piano tuner.)

If anything is wrong with a piano, make sure it is repaired before you buy it, or at least get an estimate for repair. Otherwise, you may find that the repairs make your 'bargain' cost as much as a new piano.

Now, some other hints to help you judge the quality of pianos:

WEIGHT. In general, heavy pianos are the best pianos — they last longer and stay in tune better than lighter weight pianos. Much of the weight of a piano is due to the cast iron frame which takes the tension of the strings. The frame needs to be very strong to avoid distortion which could put the strings out of tune.

Do not be persuaded to buy a lightweight piano, even though it may seem cheaper. Any cost saving could be spent having the piano tuned more frequently than a better instrument.

THE KEYS. A piano should have a full-size 88 note keyboard — 52 white keys and 36 black keys. Smaller pianos could limit your playing.

THE ACTION. If you are thinking about buying an upright, your best choice is a piano which has a 'full-size direct-blow action'. (The 'action' is the name given to all the different moving parts which make the hammers strike the strings when keys are pushed down.)

Full-size direct-blow actions are standard on most upright, studio and console pianos. They have a smooth, light, easy touch which wears better and is likely to require less adjustment than the 'drop actions' used on some consoles and most spinet pianos. Ask to see the specification of any pianos which interest you, to find out which type of action is used. (This comment does not apply to grand pianos — they have a different type of action.)

STRINGS. A piano should have a full set of about 230 strings — two copper-wound strings for each of the lower 'bass' notes, and three plain wire strings for each of the higher sounding 'treble' notes. Avoid pianos which have only two strings for each of the higher 'treble' notes.

HAMMERS. Although you may not have much choice of different types of hammers, it is best to avoid pianos with hammers which are chemically reinforced to 'last forever'. These types of hammers are usually far too hard to give a piano a pleasing, mellow tone.

SOUNDBOARD. The size and quality of the soundboard is very important if a piano is to have a good tone and volume. A good soundboard will be large, have a well-designed 'crown' (curvature) and be made of the finest materials. It is generally agreed by experts that the very best soundboards are made of close-grained spruce and, contrary to the sales pitches given for some cheap pianos, they are not made of laminated wood.

PEDALS. All pianos have at least two pedals, and some have an extra third middle pedal. Check that each pedal works smoothly and silently as described on page 11. Note: It is not normally worth paying extra for a piano because it has three pedals instead of two, as the middle pedal is not often used by most pianists.

HOW IT SOUNDS. How a piano sounds is most important, because the sound is the end result by which everything else is judged. A good piano has a mellow rounded tone — a piano should not sound bright or jangling.

Ask for a demonstration of several pianos of the same type and size, and listen with the top of each piano opened. The difference in sound quality between pianos is most obvious in the very lowest and very highest notes. The low notes should sound deep and resonant, the high notes should sound clear but not at all harsh. The piano with the clearest sounding bass and treble notes and the most mellow tone is probably the best.

A piano should have an even tone throughout the keyboard. Play all the notes on the piano. Start with the lowest notes at the left of the keyboard and move up one note at a time to the highest notes at the right of the keyboard. There should be no sudden change in tone or volume (loudness) from one note to the next.

Also compare the volume of the lowest and highest notes with the volume of notes in the middle of the keyboard. There is always some difference in volume, but pianos with the least difference are likely to be better instruments.

THE PIANO CASE OR CABINET. The outside 'case' of the piano is last on the list of features because it should be a less important consideration when buying a piano than any of the other parts. The 'case' has no real effect on the piano as a musical instrument. It is a piece of furniture which can be modelled on almost any style — modern, classical, French, and so on. The more elaborate the design, the more the piano will cost — but the outside case will not make the piano any better *as a musical instrument.*

Choose any design you like, but do not be fooled by a piano which has a good-looking case covering up a poor quality instrument — it may cost more than a far better piano inside a plainer case. Also beware of elaborate furniture designs which may go out of style during the life of the piano and reduce its value.

The quality of the finish of the case is important, because it must stand up to years of use. The best cases are made of solid wood covered with two or more layers of veneer for strength and finished with several coats of varnish or lacquer.

The hints given on the previous pages should help you to choose the best quality piano for the price you can afford. Here are a few other things you should bear in mind when you go to buy your piano:

Insist on buying the actual piano you have seen and played in the store.
You know how good this piano is, and can be sure it has had time to settle down in normal surroundings. Do not be persuaded to accept any instrument which you have not seen and played. The 'perfect piano which is still in its packing case' could be sitting in a damp warehouse, or could take months to arrive from the manufacturer!

Have the tuning checked.
The piano should be in tune to 'concert pitch' when you buy it. Ask for the tuning to be checked while you are there — it is easy for dealer to do this with a tuning fork.

Make sure the piano comes complete with a suitable piano stool or bench.

Make sure you are given a printed 'guarantee' for the piano.
Every new piano should come with a printed 'Guarantee' and a booklet from the makers which explains how to take care of your piano. Read these carefully when you get home, and make sure you conform with all the requirements, or you may invalidate the maker's or dealer's guarantee.

Ask for a written receipt.
Insist upon a full written receipt when you buy a new or secondhand piano, and keep it in a safe place — you may need it for insurance purposes.

Arrange delivery and re-tuning.
Ask for the piano to be delivered quickly so you can start enjoying it. Also arrange for it to be re-tuned one month after delivery when it has had time to settle in its new surroundings. Ask if this first tuning and any initial adjustments are included in the price of the piano — they often are!

(After the first tuning, the piano should be re-tuned every three months in its first year — unless the maker's booklet states otherwise.)

Increase your household insurance.
When you get home, give your insurance company full details of the piano, including the price, and have it added to your household policy to make sure it is properly covered. Alternatively, your piano dealer may be able to offer you a special piano insurance.

Starting to play

The way you sit and position your arms and hands is very important, because it affects how well and how easily you are able to play.

Your back should always be straight, leaning forward slightly with your shoulders relaxed.

Your upper arms should be vertical, your forearms and hands should make a straight horizontal line when your fingertips are resting on the keys.

Above all, feel comfortable and relaxed whenever you sit at your piano.

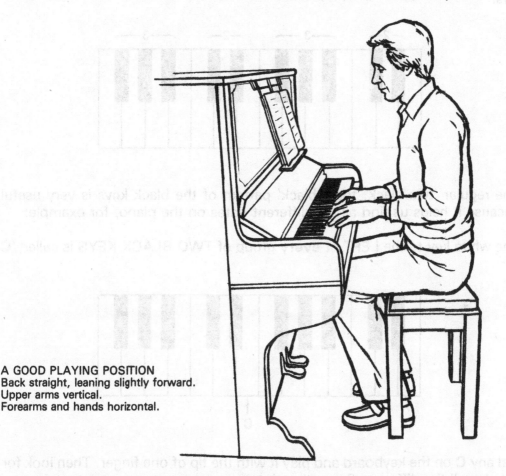

A GOOD PLAYING POSITION
Back straight, leaning slightly forward.
Upper arms vertical.
Forearms and hands horizontal.

Stand this book on the piano's music rack and sit on your piano stool or seat facing the middle of the keyboard. Move the seat backwards or forwards until your upper arm is vertical when your fingertips are on the keys. Sit on a firm cushion if your seat is not high enough for your forearms and hands to be straight and horizontal. *Then read on...*

AT THE KEYBOARD

Sit facing the middle of the keyboard, as explained on the previous page, while you continue to read. Your piano stool should be correctly placed, and you should sit in the proper position for playing, but with your hands resting on your knees for the moment. Make sure you feel comfortable sitting at the piano, because you will learn more quickly and play better when you are relaxed.

All the notes on the piano are arranged in a regular pattern of white and black keys. The white keys run right across the piano without stopping, the black keys are in alternating groups of two and three keys. *Look down at the keyboard, and count each group of black keys from left to right.* See how the black keys make a regular pattern of 'two-black, three-black' among the white keys.

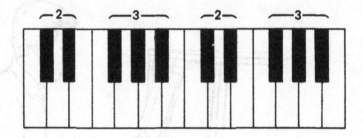

The regular 'two-black, three-black' pattern of the black keys is very useful, because it helps us find all the different notes on the piano, for example:

The white key to the LEFT of **every** group of TWO BLACK KEYS is called **'C'**

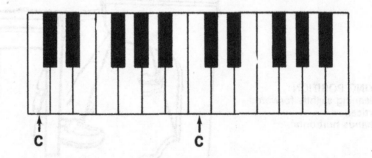

Find any **C** on the keyboard and play it with the tip of one finger. Then look for and play all the different **C**s on the piano.
Use a right-hand finger to play the higher-sounding Cs to the right of the keyboard, and a left-hand finger to play the lower-sounding Cs to the left. Play with your fingers slightly curved, as shown at the top of the next page.

24

PLAY WITH THE FINGERTIPS
— THE FINGERS SHOULD BE SLIGHTLY CURVED

All the notes played on the white keys are named after the first seven letters of the alphabet:

$$A-B-C-D-E-F-G$$

After G, the note names start again with A:

$$A-B-C-D-E-F-G-A-B-C \text{ — and so on.}$$
$$1 \quad 2 \quad 3 \quad 4 \quad 5 \quad 6 \quad 7 \quad 8$$

As you can see, after every seven notes there is another note with the same name. Notes are given the same names because they sound very much alike, in spite of being 'higher' or 'lower' than each other.

Find and play any C. Then play the C which is the eighth note to the right. Notice how similar these two notes sound, even though the second note is higher than the first note.

Remember the position of the Cs, and you can find all of the other notes — because they run in alphabetical order, from left to right:
D is the white key to the right of every C. *Find and play every D.* (There are seven Ds on a full-size piano.)

E is the white key to the right of every D. *Find and play every E.*

F is the white key to the right of every E. *Find and play every F.*

G is the white key to the right of every F. *Find and play every G.*

Then, A is the white key to the right of every G. (Remember, after G, the note names start again with A!) *Find and play every A.*

B is on the white key to the right of every A. *Find and play every B.*

Finally, C is the white key to the right of every B.

Remember that each note is always in the same place within the black and white pattern of the keys, and you will soon find your way easily around the keyboard.

Find and play each note as you read this .

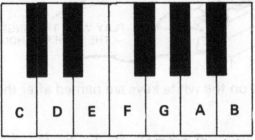

C is always to the LEFT of every group of TWO black keys.

D is always to the MIDDLE of every group of TWO black keys.

E is always to the RIGHT of every group of TWO black keys.

F is always to the LEFT of every group of THREE black keys.

G and A are always together in every group of THREE black keys, with A to the right of every G.

And B is to the RIGHT of every group of THREE black keys.

Starting with any C, play the notes on each white key to the right, one after the other, until you come to another C. Say the name of each note as you play it, and notice where it fits in the black and white pattern of the keys:

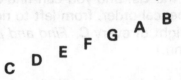

'SCALE OF C'
PLAYED UPWARDS

Then, play the same notes again in the opposite order, and say the name of each note as you play it:

'SCALE OF C'
PLAYED DOWNWARDS
        C
          B
            A
              G
                F
                  E
                    D
                      C

As you know, notes sound loudly when keys are struck firmly, and softly when keys are struck gently. However, most playing should be somewhere in between, at a medium level which is neither loud nor soft. Try to play evenly, so your notes sound at the same medium volume.

Another hint. Keep each key pressed down until you are ready to play the next, so each note lasts longer, and your playing sounds smoother.

Now, play the 'Scale' of notes from one C to the next C as smoothly and evenly as possible. Play a 'Scale' to the right of the keyboard with a right-hand finger. Next, play another 'Scale' of **C** on the left of the keyboard, with a left-hand finger. Say the name of each note to yourself as you play it.

Then, play the same notes in a different order:

C E G F G A B G D C

PLAYING WITH A BEAT

Sit at your piano, relaxed but ready to play, and start counting slowly and evenly:

1 — 2 — 3 — 4 — 1 — 2 — 3 — 4 — 1 — 2 — 3 — 4 —

Count each '1' a little more strongly to set rhythm. If you like, you can tap your foot lightly in time with your counting.

Now, play any note with a right-hand finger, every time you count '1'.
When you can do this without hesitating at all, play the note everytime you count '1' and '3'. Finally, count very slowly and evenly and play the note on every beat: 1 — 2 — 3 — 4, and so on. Repeat *all* of this, playing a note with a left-hand finger.

Next, try playing different notes in time with the beat which you count. First with a right-hand finger, and then with a left-hand finger:

PLAY:	C	D	E	F	G	F	E	D	C		
COUNT:	1	2	3	4	1	2	3	4	1	2	3	4

Keep your finger on the last **C**, so the note continues to sound while you count four beats.

You have covered a great deal in the last five pages. Read them again, next time you play, to make sure you understand everything.

Starting to play tunes

Now you have begun to find your way around the piano and have started to count the beat for music, you are ready to play some easy tunes.

Your first tunes are all played on the white keys which are in the middle of the keyboard.

Find and play the **C** *which is nearest the middle of the keyboard.* This note is called **MIDDLE C**. ('Middle C' is immediately in front of you — to the left of a group of two black keys — when you are sitting in the correct position facing the middle of the piano.)

Now, play Middle **C** *and the seven 'white' notes to the right of it with a right-hand finger.* Say the name of each note as you play it.

*Then, play Middle '**C**' and the seven 'white' notes to the left of it with a left-hand finger.* Say the name of each note as you play it.

When you have done this, you will have played three Cs, two Ds, two Es, and so on. When you play tunes, you need to know exactly which notes to play. So, for the moment, we will use small 'lower case' letters to name Middle C and notes to the right, and large 'capital' letters for notes to the left of Middle C—

NOTES IN THE MIDDLE OF THE KEYBOARD

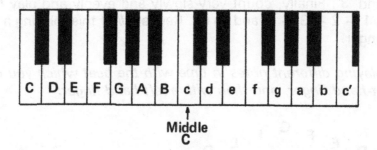

Use this drawing of the middle of the keyboard to find notes for the tunes on the facing page.

(The eighth note above Middle **C** is marked c' so you can tell it from Middle C.)

Count slowly and evenly, tap your foot in time with the beat, and play the tune which follows. Notice how a thin line is drawn between each set of 4 beats to make the notes and counting easier to read. Do not slow down at these 'Bar-Lines', but count evenly 1 2 3 4 1 2 3 4 as if they were not there. Slowly count the extra beats at the beginning to set your speed.

A SIMPLE TUNE
Play it with a right-hand finger.

				a		
			f	g f	g f	
RIGHT HAND		e	e		e	
	c	d			d	c
COUNT	1 2 3 4	1 2 3 4	1 2 3 4	1 2 3 4	1 2 3 4

Notice how a 'Double Bar-Line' (   ) marks the end of the music.

(Did you play the correct **g** and **a**? These notes are next to each other, as you will see on the keyboard drawing on the facing page.)

Some notes last longer than others in the tunes which follow. This is no problem if you count slowly and evenly, and play each note in time with the beat which is shown for it. (Keep the key for each note pressed down until the next note is to be played. Then, every note will last for the correct number of beats.)

SKIP TO MY LOU — An American Folk Song
You can see here how the words of the song fit the tune. Count the beat slowly, making each '1' a little stronger to set the rhythm.

RIGHT HAND		e e		e e	g —		d d	
			c c					B B
COUNT	1 2 3 4	1 2 3 4	1 2 3 4	1 2 3 4

Lost my part-ner what'll I do__ lost my part-ner

d d	f__	e e		e e	g —	d d e d	c__ c__
			c c				
1 2 3 4	1 2 3 4	1 2 3 4	1 2 3 4	1 2 3 4

what'll I do__ Lost my part-ner what'll I do__ Skip to my Lou, my dar - ling __.

(Notice that **B** is the note to the left of **Middle C**.)

29

The drawing of the keyboard is repeated here to help you find the notes for the tunes on this page.

NOTES IN THE MIDDLE OF THE KEYBOARD

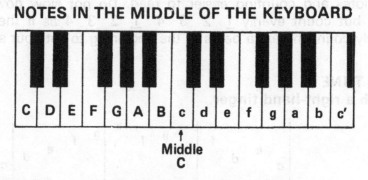

C D E F G A B c d e f g a b c'

↑
Middle C

BOBBY SHAFTOE — An English and American Folk Song
Play this tune with a right-hand finger.

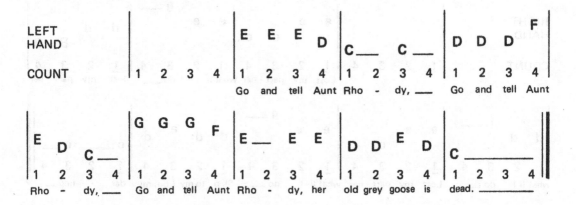

Play the next tune with a *left-hand* finger:

GO AND TELL AUNT RHODY — An American Folk Song

Practise these tunes until you can play smoothly in time with the beat.

Playing with all your fingers

This next step will help you to play more smoothly and allow you to start playing with both hands at the same time.

From now on, you should be especially relaxed and patient with yourself, because you will be using your fingers in new ways. Pay attention to all the instructions and hints, and make sure you can play everything correctly before going on.

THUMB AND FINGER NUMBERS
The thumb and fingers of each hand are given numbers for piano playing.

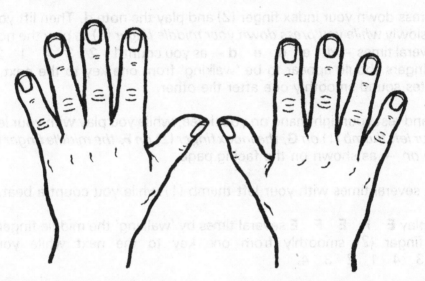

Remember that the thumb is always '1' — the fingers are '2', '3', '4', and '5'. Learn this numbering so you will know which finger to use for each note. (Be very careful if you play another instrument, because piano fingering may not be the same.)

TAKE CARE OF YOUR HANDS
Keep your fingernails fairly short so they do not hit the keys when you play — it is best if your nails are filed level with the fingertips.

Wash your hands before you play — to keep the piano keys clean.

Never try to play with cold hands — because your fingers will be stiff

Flex your fingers before you play to make them supple. You can loosen your finger joints by clenching your hand into a tight fist and throwing it away from you, so the fingers fly open and outstretched. *Try it.*

Sit relaxed at your piano, and rest your right-hand thumb and fingers lightly on the keys — as shown on the facing page. Your thumb (1) should be on Middle C, your index finger (2) should be on **d**, your middle finger (3) on **e**, and so on. (Do not put your left hand on the keys at the moment — let it rest on your left knee.)

Your whole right hand should be relaxed and resting so lightly that none of the keys are pressed down. Each of your fingers should be slightly curved, but the thumb should be straight.

Now, play Middle C several times by moving your thumb (1) up and down slowly as you count a beat — 1 2 3 4 1 2 3 4

Next press down your index finger (2) and play the note **d**. Then lift your index finger slowly *while you press down your middle finger* (3) to play the note **e**. Do this several times — **d e d e d** — as you count 1 2 3 4 1 2 3 4. Your fingers should appear to be 'walking' from one key to the next, making the notes sound smoothly one after the other.

Relax and rest your right hand on your knee, while you play with your left hand. *Put your left thumb* (1) *on* **G**, *the index finger* (2) *on* **F**, *the middle finger* (3) *on* **E**, *and so on* — as shown on the facing page.

Play G several times with your left thumb (1) while you count a beat.

Then play **E F E F E** several times by 'walking' the middle finger (3) and index finger (2) smoothly from one key to the next while you count 1 2 3 4 1 2 3 4.

TRAINING YOUR FINGERS
Practise this for a few minutes every time you play to train your fingers to move independently. Walk your fingers from one key to the next to make your playing smooth and professional sounding. Play each hand separately at first, then play with both hands at the same time. Start very slowly, and try to make each note sound equally loudly—

RIGHT HAND
FINGER	1	2	3	4	5	4	3	2	1
NOTE	c	d	e	f	g	f	e	d	c

LEFT HAND
FINGER	1	2	3	4	5	4	3	2	1
NOTE	G	F	E	D	C	D	E	F	G

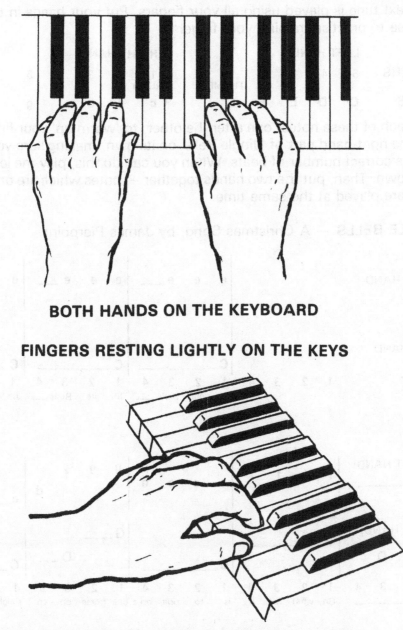

BOTH HANDS ON THE KEYBOARD

FINGERS RESTING LIGHTLY ON THE KEYS

THUMB STRAIGHT, FINGERS SLIGHTLY CURVED.
PLAY WITH THE FINGERTIPS

IMPORTANT

You can practise moving your fingers as explained opposite whenever you have a spare moment, even if you are away from a piano. Rest your thumbs and fingertips lightly on any firm surface and practise moving one finger after the other while counting to yourself. Flex your fingers before and after you do this to loosen up the joints.

The next tune is played using all your fingers. Put your hands in the positions you use to practise training your fingers—

	LEFT HAND					RIGHT HAND				
FINGERS	5	4	3	2	1 THUMB	1 THUMB	2	3	4	5
NOTES	C	D	E	F	G	c	d	e	f	g

Play each of these notes, one after the other, to 'warm up' your fingers. Then, play the right-hand part of 'Jingle Bells' on its own, making sure you give each note its correct number of beats. When you can do this, play the left-hand part on its own. Then, put the two hands together — notes which are one above the other are played at the same time.

JINGLE BELLS — A Christmas Song, by James Pierpoint

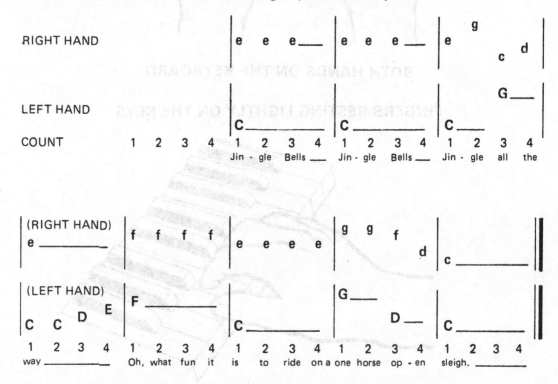

Try to keep your eyes on the book and play without looking down at the keys. As long as your fingers are in the right places and you use the correct fingers, you will play the right notes.

Take a few moments to think about a tune before you play it. Sing or hum the first notes to yourself, so you get the right feeling for the tune, and start counting and playing at the proper speed.

How to practise

Try to practise every day for at least twenty minutes. Regular daily practice is far better than playing for several hours once or twice a week. The more often you play, the better you will become, and the more enjoyment you will get out of your music.

If possible, choose times when you can be on your own for practising. Nothing is worse than others listening while you are learning to play.

Be patient. Make sure you can play each piece smoothly at the right speed before going on to the next tune. However, try to learn something new every week, even if it is just a simple tune.

Start playing everything slowly. When you can play correctly and evenly, gradually work up to the proper speed. You will never play well if you try to play quickly too soon.

Relax while you are playing. Give your fingers a rest now and then, and stop playing for a while if they become tired or stiff.

Do not be discouraged if your playing does not always seem to be improving very quickly. As long as you practise regularly, learn new things and keep trying to improve, your playing will gradually become better all the time.

Plan your practising to make the best of your time, like this:

1. Flex your fingers to loosen them. Warm your hands if they are cold.

2. Practise playing the 'finger training' patterns shown on page 32. This will help you to gain better control of your fingers. Make sure you play these patterns smoothly and evenly.

3. Practise something new, or something which you do not play well. If part of a tune seems awkward or slows down your playing, practise it separately for a few minutes every day until you can play it smoothly. Then go back and try to play the whole tune smoothly right through.

4. Finally play music you already know. Try to polish your playing by correcting any mistakes, even when you are playing for fun, so you will not get into any bad habits.

Starting to read music

Learning to read music is much easier than most people think. There is no real mystery about it — a piece of music is simply a set of instructions which tells you how to play a particular tune. Different signs tell you everything about the music — which notes to play, when and how to play them and how long they should sound.

Already you know more than you may realise about music. You know the names of the notes on the white keys, and have learned to play them in time with beats which you count. The rest is not difficult.

Of course, you could learn to play the piano without reading music — if you have an exceptional flair, or want to restrict yourself to simple tunes. However, you will be able to learn new tunes more easily, quickly and correctly, if you take a little time to learn to read music. Now is the best time for you to learn, and take the next step towards becoming a good pianist.

HOW MUSIC IS WRITTEN

Musical notes are written on sets of lines called 'staves'. Each line and space on the staves is like a step on a musical ladder — one note is on the line, the next note higher is in the space above and so on. The higher the note sounds, the higher it is on the stave.

Music for the piano is written on two staves joined by a bracket. Two staves are needed because there are so many notes on the piano.

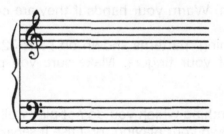

HIGHER NOTES
— usually played by the right hand

LOWER NOTES
— usually played by the left hand

The *upper* stave is for notes on the right of the keyboard which are usually played by the right hand.

The *lower* stave is for notes on the left of the keyboard which are usually played by the left hand.

(Notes in the very middle of the keyboard can be on either stave, as you will see.)

At the beginning of every line of music there is a sign called a 'Clef':

 on each of upper line of piano music, and 𝄢 on each lower line.

Clefs help us to read music by marking the position of one note on each stave.

The 'Treble Clef' or 'G Clef' marks the position of the note 'g' on the second line up:

G CLEF

POSITION OF NOTE 'g'
ON 2ND LINE

As long as you remember the position of 'g', you can work out all the other notes which are usually played by the right hand:

'g' is on the second line, the next note higher — 'a' — is in the space above, 'b' is on the middle line, and so on. Going downwards, 'f' is in the space below 'g' then 'e' is on the bottom line, and 'd' is below the bottom line. Then, the next note lower — Middle C — is on a short line below the stave.

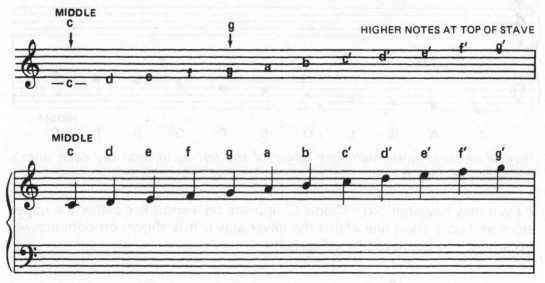

This is how these notes appear in music —

The 'stems' of notes can go up (♩) or down (♩) — it does not make any difference to the notes.

Play all these notes with one finger of the right hand saying the note's name as you play it. Start with Middle C and play each white key to the right.

Another Clef is used on the lower stave of piano music:

 — the 'Bass Clef' or 'F Clef' marks the position of the note **F** on the second line down. The big 'dot' of the F Clef marks the note:

F CLEF

POSITION OF NOTE **'F'**
ON 2ND LINE FROM TOP OF STAVE

As long as you remember the position of 'F', you can work out all the other notes which are usually played by the left hand.

'**F**' is on the second line from the top, '**G**' is in the top space and '**A**' is on the top line. Going down, '**E**' is in the space below '**F**', then '**D**' is on the middle line, and so on.

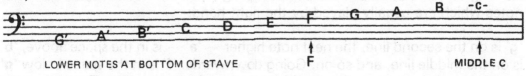

LOWER NOTES AT BOTTOM OF STAVE   F   MIDDLE C

This is how the notes appear in music:

G'   A'   B'   C   D   E   F   G   A   B   MIDDLE C

Play all of these notes with one finger of the left hand, and say each note's name as you play it.

As you may have noticed, 'Middle C' appears on a short line *below* the upper stave *and* on a short line *above* the lower stave. It is shown on both staves, because it can be played by either hand.

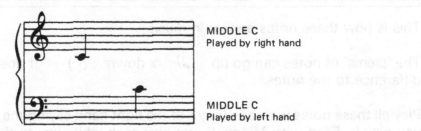

MIDDLE C
Played by right hand

MIDDLE C
Played by left hand

You can play the next few tunes with the notes shown here. *Rest your fingers lightly on the keys before you start to play. Make sure each finger is on the correct key.* Your right thumb should be on Middle C, your left thumb should be on **G**. Then play each of these notes in turn:

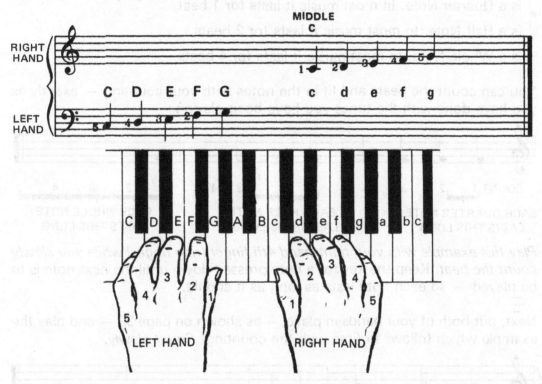

The small numbers in front of notes on the staves tell you which finger to use to play each note: 1 = thumb, 2 = index finger, and so on.

Try to keep your eyes on the music while you play the next tune. Put your hands in place, then concentrate on reading the notes and pressing down the correct finger without watching your hands.

MUSICAL ECHOES

COUNT 1 2 3 4   1 2 3 4   1 2 3 4   1 2 3 4

As you know from the tunes you have been playing, some notes last for more beats than other notes. In music, the *shape* of a note tells us how many beats it should last.

♩ is a Quarter Note. In most music it lasts for 1 beat.

♪ is a Half Note. In most music it lasts for 2 beats.

𝅝 is a Whole Note. In most music it lasts for 4 beats.

You can count the beats and fit in the notes with your counting — exactly as you have done with the tunes you have been playing.

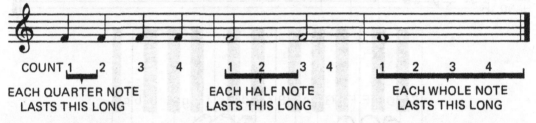

COUNT 1 2 3 4   1 2 3 4   1 2 3 4

EACH QUARTER NOTE   EACH HALF NOTE   EACH WHOLE NOTE
LASTS THIS LONG   LASTS THIS LONG   LASTS THIS LONG

Play this example with your right-hand 4th finger (ring finger) while you slowly count the beat. Keep the key for a note pressed down until the next note is to be played — so each note lasts as long as it should.

Next, put both of your hands in place — as shown on page 39 — and play the example which follows in time with the counting. *Count slowly.*

COUNT 1 2 3 4   1 2 3 4   1 2 3 4   1 2 3 4

Make sure you play smoothly without slowing down at the 'Bar-Lines'. *Then, play the next example with both hands together. Remember: notes which are one above the other are played at the same time.*

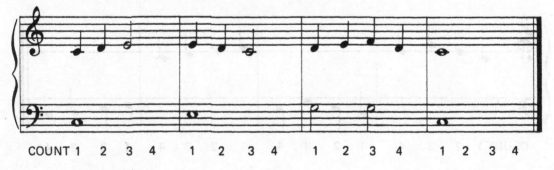

COUNT 1 2 3 4   1 2 3 4   1 2 3 4   1 2 3 4

Now you can use what you have learned to play a tune from music.

ODE TO JOY by Beethoven
Notice that the first, second and fourth lines are almost the same — only the ends are different. Position your hands as shown on page 39, and count slowly
<u>1</u> 2 3 4 to set the speed before you start.

I KNOW WHERE I'M GOING — An Irish and English Folk Song

As you can see from the fingering numbers in front of the first notes, this tune starts with the right thumb (1) on Middle C, and the left little finger (5) on the C below — the same positions as on page 39.

The second half of this tune is the same as the first — except at the end.

1 2 3 4   1 2 3 4   1 2 3 4   1 2 3 4
I know where I'm   go · ing   and   I know who's going with me   Oh,

1 2 3 4   1 2 3 4   1 2 3 4   1 2 3 4
I know who I   love   but I don't know who I'll   mar · ry   Now

1 2 3 4   1 2 3 4   1 2 3 4   1 2 3 4
I have shirt of   silk   and shoes of fin · est lea · ther,   But

1 2 3 4   1 2 3 4   1 2 3 4   1 2 3 4
I would trade them   all   to be with my true   lov   er.

42

Starting to play chords

A 'chord' is the sound which is made when two or more notes are played at the same time. Chords can be played with either hand, or with both hands together. Chords are used in piano music to add 'harmony' to give a full-sounding 'backing' to melodies.

RIGHT HAND CHORDS

Try this. Put your right hand on the keyboard in the position you have been using. *Then, press down the thumb (1) and the middle finger (3) at the same time,* to play 'Middle C' and '**e**' together. The notes should be played at *exactly* the same time, and sound equally loudly. *Try playing these notes together several times.*

As you know, in music, notes which are played at the same time are shown one note above the other. So, the chord you have played looks like this.

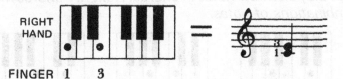

Now, try using different fingers to play different chords:

First, play 'c' and 'e' with the thumb (1) and middle finger (3), as you have already done.

Next, play 'e' and 'g' with the middle finger (3) and little finger (5).

Then, play 'd' and 'f' with the index finger (2) and ring finger (4).

Finally, play 'c' and 'e' again with the thumb and middle finger.

Play each chord four times while you slowly count a beat. Make sure all notes sound equally loud. *Then, rest your hand.*

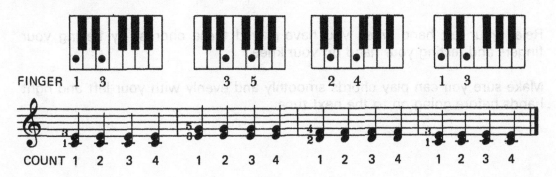

LEFT HAND CHORDS

Chords can also be played with the left hand. *Try this:*

Rest your left-hand fingers lightly on the keys, with the thumb (1) on G below Middle C — as shown on page 39. Then, play these two-note chords. (Make sure the notes of each chord are played equally loudly and sound at exactly the same time.) *Play each chord twice.*

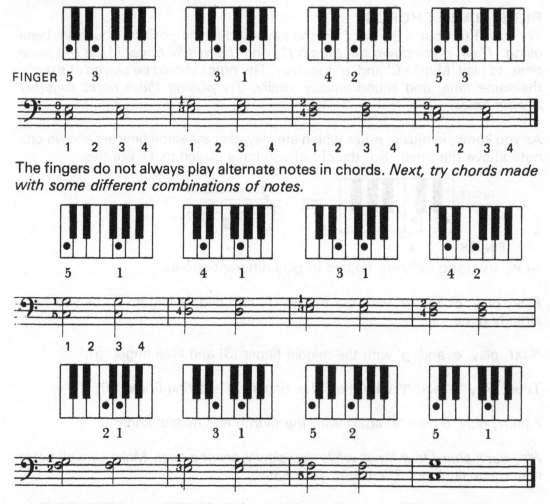

The fingers do not always play alternate notes in chords. *Next, try chords made with some different combinations of notes.*

Relax your left hand when you have played these chords, by flexing your fingers and resting your hand on your knee.

Make sure you can play chords smoothly and evenly with your left and right hands before going on to the next tune.

See how much more interesting 'Jingle Bells' sounds when a few chords are added to the melody.

JINGLE BELLS
Follow all the notes and fingering very carefully so you play correctly.

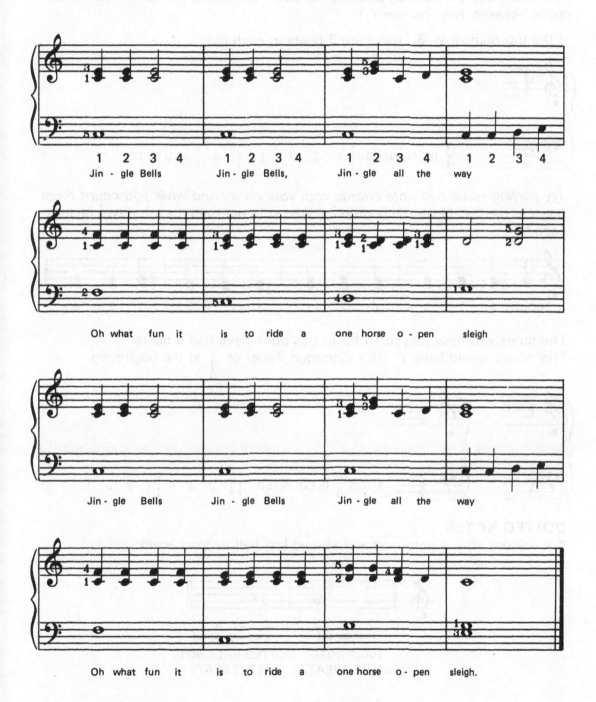

More about music

At the beginning of every piece of music, there are two numbers, or a sign —
C — next to each of the clefs. This is the 'time signature', which tells us
how many beats should be counted for each 'bar' in the music. (A 'bar' is the
space between two 'bar-lines'.)

If the top number is '3', there are 3 beats in each bar.

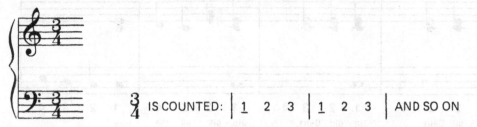

*Try playing some two-note chords with your right hand while you count three
beats to the bar.* Make the first beat a little stronger than the other two beats in
each bar.

The tunes you have played so far in this book have had 4 beats.
This music would have C (for Common Time) or $\frac{4}{4}$ at the beginning:

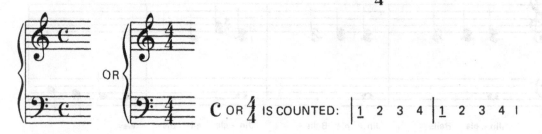

DOTTED NOTES

A small dot after a note means it should last half as long again:

TIED NOTES
A note is often made longer by joining it to the next note with a curved line called a 'tie'. Then, the note is played once, but it lasts for the total number of beats of the notes 'tied' together.

NOTE LASTS THIS LONG   NOTE LASTS THIS LONG

This only applies if the next note has the *same name and position*.

SLURS
Curved lines over or under two or more *different* notes mean these notes should be played smoothly:

= play smoothly   = play smoothly

Play the next tune — it will help you learn to recognise all of the musical signs explained on these two pages.

DRINK TO ME ONLY WITH THINE EYES — Traditional song
Count slowly 1—2—3—, before you start playing.

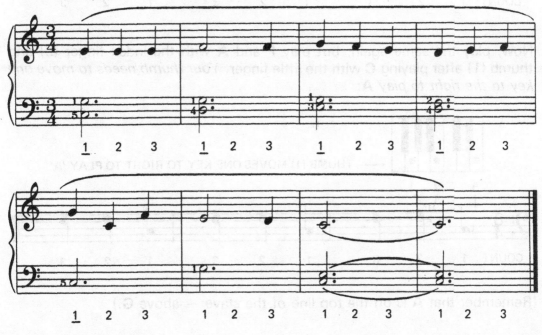

More interesting left-hand parts

So far you have used your left hand to add two-note chords or single 'bass' notes to the melodies of tunes you have played. In this next step, you will put the two together, so you play bass notes *and* harmony under a melody. This adds rhythm to a tune, and makes the left hand part more interesting. *Try this:*

Rest your left-hand fingers lightly on the keys with the thumb (1) on **G** and the little finger (5) on **C**. Then, follow these instructions:

1. Play **C** with your little finger (5).
2. Play **E** and **G** together with your middle finger (3) and the thumb (1), *lifting your little finger off C as the other fingers press down.*
3. Play **E** and **G** together again.

Do this several times, while you slowly count <u>1</u> 2 3 <u>1</u> 2 3

Now, play the same again, but play **F** and **A** with the index finger (2) and thumb (1) after playing **C** with the little finger. *Your thumb needs to move one key to the right to play* **A**:

(Remember that **A** is on the top line of the stave — above **G**.)

Next, play **D** with your 4th finger, followed by **F** and **G** together played with the index finger (2) and thumb (1). Notice how the thumb must move back to the left of **A** to play **G**:

Now, play all of these bass notes and chords together. *Read each note and finger number very carefully, to make sure you play the right notes with the correct fingers.* Start slowly and count evenly.

When you can play this smoothly, without slowing down to play different notes or chords, play the tune on the next page.

BEAUTIFUL, BEAUTIFUL BROWN EYES — An American Folk Song

Play the melody (right-hand part) first, so you know how it goes. Then play the left hand and right hand together. Notice how the left-hand notes change every two bars. Count slowly 1 2 3 1 2 3 to set the speed and rhythm before you start playing.

50

MORE LEFT-HAND NOTES

We will now start moving the left hand to other places on the keyboard to play chords with different notes.

Try this—

Play **C** with the left-hand little finger (5). Then —

Move your hand one key to the left, and play **B** with the little finger.

Move left another key, to play **A** with the little finger.

Finally, another key to the left to play **G** with the little finger.

Now, play these notes again, but this time move your whole hand back to play **E** and **G** together after each note:

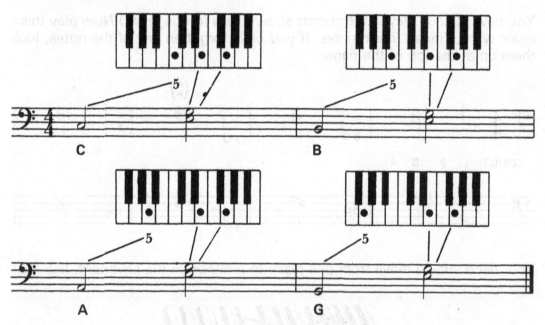

Do this a few times, saying the name of each 'bass' note as you play it. Then practise playing **C**, chord, **G**, chord, several times—

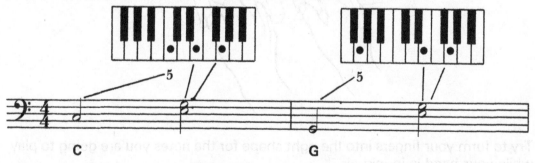

Keep repeating this — **C**, chord, **G**, chord, **C**, chord, **G**, chord until you can play it evenly.

51

LEFT-HAND NOTES

Here are the left-hand notes you have played so far, plus another **F** which is below the bottom line of the stave, and **B** above the stave:

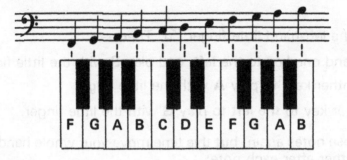

You have already played the chords shown here (on page 49.) Now play them again with different 'bass' notes. If you have forgotten any of the notes, look them up at the top of the page.

Your hand should move from one place to another on the keyboard, like this:

Try to form your fingers into the right shape for the notes you are going to play while your hand is in mid-air.

Play this next tune to practise bass notes with chords:

EARLY EVENING
This tune is in $\frac{3}{4}$ time, so you should slowly count 1 2 3 1 2 3 to set the speed and rhythm before you start playing. (Notice that the chords are played twice after each bass note.)

Rests

In many pieces of music there are a few beats when one hand plays while the other 'rests'. In some music, both hands may rest for a few silent beats. Rests are counted in exactly the same way as notes:

The 'Whole Note Rest' can also show a whole bar's rest.

Play and count this example to learn how Rests work—

LEFT HAND RESTS

In some tunes, the first and last bars do not have the full number of beats given by the time signature. This happens because the tune starts in the middle or at the end of the first bar. In these tunes count the missing beats before you begin playing to get the timing and rhythm right.

Count and play these examples:

Counting out the 'timing' is the secret to finding out how long each note or rest should last to make the music sound right. Always start counting slowly and evenly, so you understand the timing of the tune, before trying to play at the correct speed. If a few notes seem to slow up your playing, practise them on their own until you can play them at the same speed as other parts of the tune.

Make sure you understand everything so far, before playing the next tune.

WHEN THE SAINTS GO MARCHING IN — A traditional jazz classic

Notice that this tune starts on the second beat in the first bar. Count the missing first beat to lead you in: <u>1</u> 2 3 4 <u>1</u>

COUNT (1) 2 3 4 1 2 3 4 1 2 3 4 1 2 3 4

Oh, when the saints _____ go march - ing in _____

Oh, when the saints go march - ing in, _____

Oh, how I want _____ to be in that num - ber

When the saints go march - ing in. _____

More notes to play

RIGHT-HAND NOTES

Here are the notes you have been playing with the right hand, along with some other notes which you are going to be playing from now on:

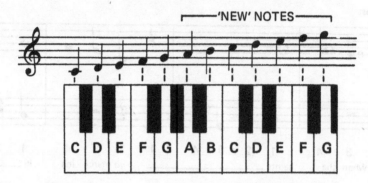

You can play different notes by moving your right hand to other parts of the keyboard in various ways. First, you can 'jump' your whole right hand to another place, in the same way you moved your left hand to play different bass notes and chords. *Try playing this. Follow the finger numbers very carefully and say the name of each note as you play it.*

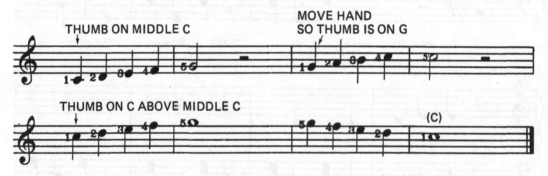

'Jumping' your whole hand is one way to move to notes which cannot be played in one place. Notes in other parts of the keyboard may also be reached by spreading your fingers, so they take bigger steps and play different notes from those they have played so far.

Here, the thumb (1) plays Middle C, then the index finger (2) plays **E**, the middle finger (3) plays **G**, and the little finger (5) ends up on the **C** above Middle C. *Play it.*

THUMB PLAYS MIDDLE C   INDEX FINGER PLAYS E   MIDDLE FINGER PLAYS G   LITTLE FINGER PLAYS HIGHER C

Now use what you have learned to play the notes shown here. (Read each note and its finger number very carefully.)

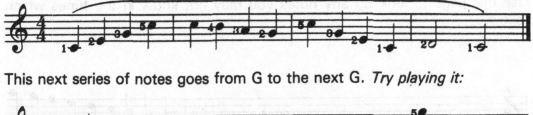

This next series of notes goes from G to the next G. *Try playing it:*

THUMB PLAYS G	INDEX FINGER PLAYS C	MIDDLE FINGER PLAYS E	LITTLE FINGER PLAYS HIGHER G

Play it again, along with some notes at the top of the stave.

The different notes you have learned here are found in many of the tunes which follow.

Are you playing correctly?

Check your playing regularly to avoid getting into any bad habits:

Are you sitting correctly at the piano when you play? See page 23.
Are your hands in a good relaxed position when you play? See page 33.
Are you playing each note with the correct finger? Follow the finger numbers — they are there to help you.
Are you reading music correctly. See pages 36-40, 46, 47 and 54.
Are you playing evenly, without quickening up or slowing down?
Do you count an even beat when you learn new tunes, so your music sounds as it should?
Do you 'walk' your fingers from note to note, so your music flows smoothly?
Do you keep your fingers on each key long enough, so each note lasts for the correct number of beats?

When was your piano last tuned? If it has not been tuned for six months, or if there is anything wrong with the piano, see pages 13-15.

If there is anything you did not understand in the book, read it again.

Notes for both hands

Use this page to look up any notes you may not know in the tunes which follow.

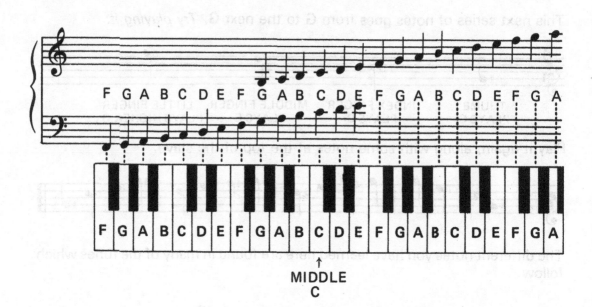

Notice that there are several notes (like Middle C) which are shown below the upper stave *and* above the lower stave on short lines (called Leger Lines). These notes may be played by either hand depending on where they are written:

When they are under the 𝄞 stave, they are usually played by the right hand.

When they are over the 𝄢 stave, they are usually played by the left hand.

AU CLAIR DE LA LUNE — A French Folk Song

Play with each hand on its own so you know how each part is played. The right hand plays in two different places — follow the fingering. The left hand plays some *three* note chords — make sure each note sounds equally loudly. Then, play both hands together. Count slowly 1 2 3 4

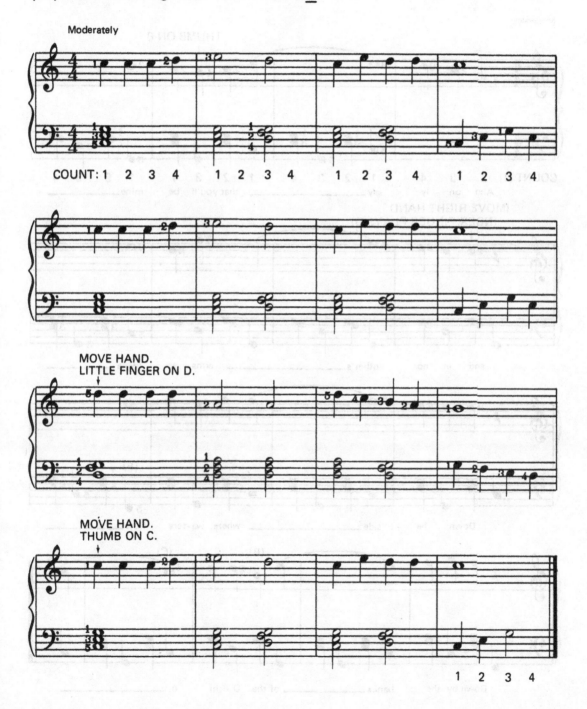

BANKS OF THE OHIO — An American Folk Song

As with most piano music, the fingering is only shown where it is not obvious — or where the hand has to move to another place. Follow the counting carefully so the tune sounds right, and look up any notes which you may not remember on page 58.

THUMB ON B

Moderately

COUNT (1) 2 3 4 | 1 2 3 4 | 1 2 3 4 | 1 2 3 4

And on - ly say _____ that you'll be mine _____

(MOVE RIGHT HAND — INDEX FINGER PLAYS D)

and in no other's _____ arms en - twine _____

(F)

Down be - side _____ where wa - ters flow _____

(B) (C)

Down by the banks _____ of the O - hi - o. _____

ON TOP OF OLD SMOKEY — An American Folk Song

Read all notes carefully, and be sure to use the correct fingering.
Play each hand separately, then play with both hands together.
This tune has three beats to the bar. Slowly count <u>1</u> 2 3 <u>1</u> 2 3 to lead
you in—

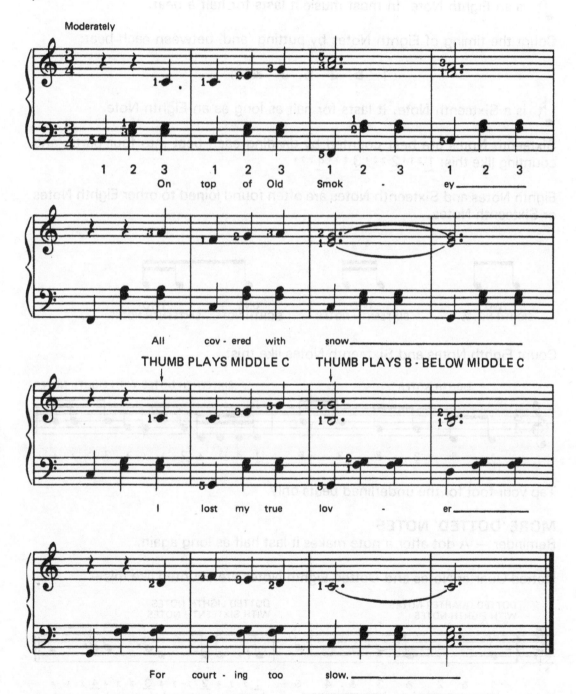

61

More Advanced Music

In many tunes you will find notes which last for less than one beat.

♪ is an Eighth Note. In most music it lasts for half a beat.

Count the timing of Eighth Notes by putting 'and' between each beat:

1 & 2 & 3 & 4

♪ is a Sixteenth Note. It lasts for half as long as an Eighth Note.

Sixteenth Notes are best counted by dividing each beat into four parts, and counting like this: 1 2 3 4 2 2 3 4 3 2 3 4 4 2 3 4

Eighth Notes and Sixteenth Notes are often found joined to other Eighth Notes or Sixteenth Notes.

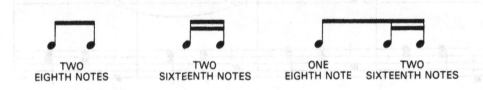

| TWO
EIGHTH NOTES | TWO
SIXTEENTH NOTES | ONE
EIGHTH NOTE | TWO
SIXTEENTH NOTES |

Count Eighth Notes and Sixteenth Notes like this:

Tap your foot for the underlined beats only.

MORE 'DOTTED' NOTES
Reminder — A dot after a note makes it last half as long again.

Dotted Quarter Notes and Dotted Eighth Notes are counted like this—

MORE RESTS

Eighth Notes Rests (♪) and Sixteenth Note Rests (♪) are counted in the same way as the notes they replace.

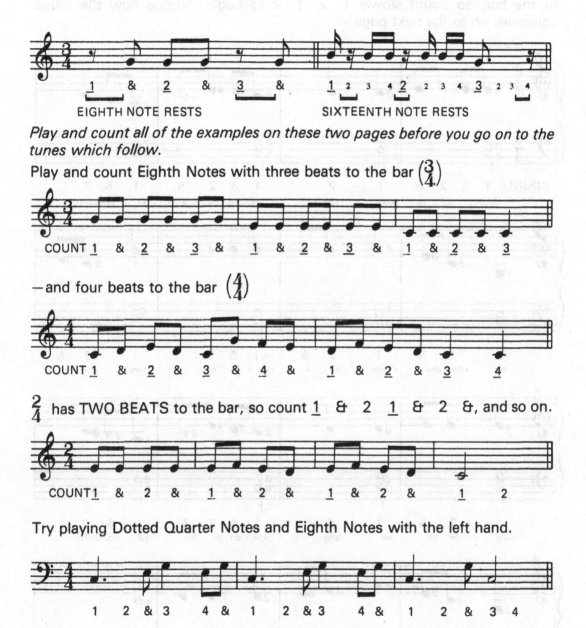

EIGHTH NOTE RESTS   SIXTEENTH NOTE RESTS

Play and count all of the examples on these two pages before you go on to the tunes which follow.

Play and count Eighth Notes with three beats to the bar $\left(\frac{3}{4}\right)$

COUNT 1 & 2 & 3 &   1 & 2 & 3 &   1 & 2 & 3

—and four beats to the bar $\left(\frac{4}{4}\right)$

COUNT 1 & 2 & 3 & 4 &   1 & 2 & 3   4

$\frac{2}{4}$ has TWO BEATS to the bar, so count 1 & 2 1 & 2 &, and so on.

COUNT 1 & 2 &   1 & 2 &   1 & 2 &   1   2

Try playing Dotted Quarter Notes and Eighth Notes with the left hand.

1   2 & 3   4 & 1   2 & 3   4 & 1   2 & 3 4

(Notice how you count 'and' only where an Eighth Note is to be played.)

Count out the beat when you first play a piece of music to get the timing right. Then play without counting when you have the feeling of the tune.

63

WALTZING MATILDA — A song from the Australian bush

Play the right-hand part on its own first. Read the notes carefully and follow the fingering. (Look up notes on 'Leger Lines' on page 58.) This tune has two beats to the bar, so count slowly 1 2 1 2 to begin. Notice how the music continues on to the next page.

64

Continued on next page

Moderato

Waltz - ing Mat - il - da___ waltz - ing Mat - il - da

you'll come a - waltz - ing Mat - il - da with me, and he

sang as he sat and wait - ed 'til his bil - ly boiled

you'll come a - waltz - ing Mat - il - da with me.___

THE RED RIVER VALLEY — A cowboy song

The left hand plays Eighth Notes as a backing to the melody of this tune. Play each hand separately, making sure every note lasts for the proper number of beats. Then, play slowly with both hands together. (Rest your left hand lightly on the keys in the right position before you start.)

Moderately

1 2 3 4 & | 1 & 2 & 3 & 4 & | 1 & 2 & 3 & 4 &
From this val - ley they say you are go - ing ———— We will

1 & 2 & 3 & 4 & | 1 & 2 & 3 & 4 &
miss —— your bright eyes and sweet smile For they

say you are tak - ing the sun - shine That has

bright - ened our way for a while.

YELLOW ROSE OF TEXAS — A song from the Southern USA

This tune has some Dotted Quarter Notes played by the right hand — follow the counting carefully to get the timing right.

Rest your left hand in position on the keys before you start to play.

(Remember: C means there are four beats to the bar.)

There's a yel-low rose of Tex-as that I am going to see no

oth-er fel-low knows her not half as well as me. She

cried so when I left her it near-ly broke my heart and

if I ev-er find her we nev-er more will part.

SILENT NIGHT — An Austrian Christmas song by Franz Gruber
Read this piece of music carefully. Notice that the right hand moves frequently
to play chords with the melody — make sure you use the correct fingering for
each note. Take your time with this tune and keep coming back to it until you
can play smoothly.

COUNT 1 2 & 3   1 2 3   1 2 & 3   1 2 3
Sil - ent Night ____   Ho - ly Night

1 2 3   1 2 3   1 2 3   1 2 3
All is calm   All is bright

1 2 3   1 2 & 3   1 2 & 3   1 2 3
'Round yon Vir - gin   Mo - ther and Child

1 2 3   1 2 & 3   1 2 & 3   1 2 3
Ho - ly In - fant so   ten - der and mild

Continued on next page

68

Sleep in heav - en - ly peace

1 2 & 3 1 2 & 3 1

sleep_____ in heav - en - ly peace._____

MICHAEL ROW THE BOAT ASHORE — A traditional Spiritual

Notice how the left hand plays some different chords and bass notes in this tune. When you come to the end of the song, play it again from the beginning.

Joyfully

(1) (2) 3 1 2 & 3 4 1 2 3 4 1 2 3 4 1 2 3 4

Mich - ael row the boat a - shore Hal - le - lu - yah. Mich - ael

1 2 & 3 4

row the boat a - shore Hal - le - lu - jah.

Playing runs of notes

So far, you have been moving around the keyboard by 'jumping' your whole hand, or spreading your fingers to reach different notes. Another way is used to play runs of notes which cannot be reached by five fingers.

THE RIGHT HAND
Runs of notes towards the right of the keyboard can be played smoothly by passing the thumb underneath the fingers, like this:

Play Middle **C, D** and **E** with the right thumb (1), index finger (2) and middle finger (3). *Then, keep your 3rd finger on E, and bring your thumb under the fingers to play* **F**.

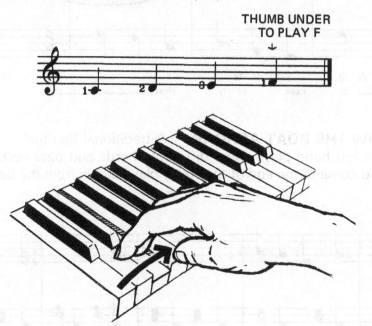

Your wrist and arm should stay as straight as possible and not twist when your thumb moves under the fingers.

Now, use this 'technique' to play a Scale of **C** as smoothly as possible, holding each note until the next is to be played. *Follow the fingering carefully:*

The right-hand fingers cross over the thumb to play runs of notes towards the left of the keyboard, like this:

Play **A, G** and **F** with the middle finger (3), index finger (2) and thumb (1).

Then, keep your thumb on **F**, *and bring the middle finger over the thumb to play* **E**. Then play **D** and Middle **C** with your index finger and thumb:

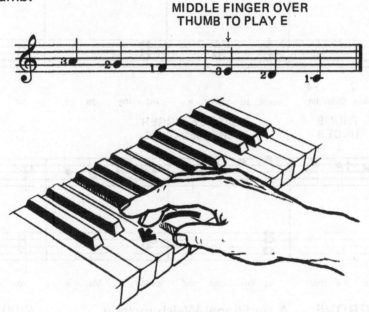

Now, play down the Scale of C as smoothly as possible, holding each note until the next is to be played. *Follow the fingering carefully:*

THE LEFT HAND
Runs of notes can be played in a similar way by the left hand. *Try this:*

Play runs with both hands for a few minutes every time you play.

Use the next tunes to practise what you have learned on the previous pages.
Follow the fingering exactly and play as smoothly and evenly as possible.

YANKEE DOODLE — An early American Folk Song

Lively

COUNT 1 2 3 4
Yan-kee Doo- dle   went to town, a - rid - ing   on a   po - ny, He

THUMB
UNDER

MIDDLE FINGER
CROSSES OVER

stuck a fea - ther   in his cap and   called it Mac - a -   ro - ni.

THE ASH GROVE — A traditional Welsh melody

MIDDLE FINGER
CROSSES OVER

Moderately

(1) (2) 3

INDEX FINGER
CROSSES OVER

CRADLE SONG — by Brahms

Gently, and not too quickly

(1) (2) 3 & 1 2 3 &

THUMB

LONDONDERRY AIR — A famous Irish melody

This tune is used for many songs, including 'Danny Boy'.

Follow the fingering carefully, and make sure all notes last for the correct number of beats. Look up the notes which are written with 'Leger Lines' on page 58.

(LITTLE FINGER ON B) (FINGERS CHANGE ON SAME NOTE)

(LITTLE FINGER ON D)

Notes on the Black Keys

So far, the music in this book has been played on the white keys of the piano using what are called the 'natural notes' — A, B, C, D, E, F and G.

Notes which are played on the black keys are called 'sharp notes' and 'flat notes' — 'sharps' and 'flats', for short.

SHARPS AND FLATS

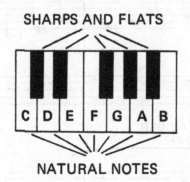

NATURAL NOTES

SHARPS (#)
A Sharp note is played on the next key to the right of the 'natural note' with the same letter name — **'C sharp'** is played on the black key to the right of **C**.

C sharp

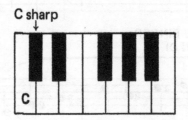

Sharp notes are marked with a sharp sign — # . (C Sharp is written C # .)

Play all the notes on the black keys, saying the name of each note as you play it. Notice how each sharp note is on the black key to the right of the natural note with the same letter name.

C# D#   F# G# A#

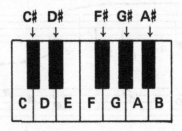

On the staves, sharp notes are shown by a sharp sign (#) in front of the note which is to be 'sharpened'

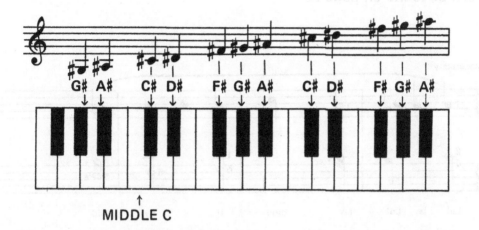

MIDDLE C

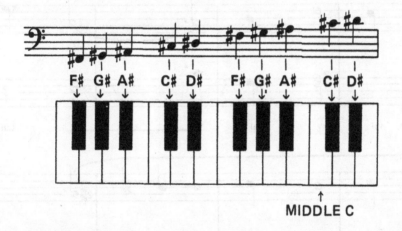

MIDDLE C

Play natural notes (on the white keys) and sharp notes (on the black keys) mixed together, before you go on to the tunes which follow.
Here, the notes on black keys have a sharp sign (#) in front of them, all other notes are natural notes played on the white keys.

COVENTRY CAROL — A Fifteenth-Century Christmas carol

Look up the sharp notes (♯) on the previous page, if you need to. All other notes can be found on page 58.

Lul - lay, Lul - lay thou ti - ny child

Bye, bye, lul - lay lul - lay_____ Lul -

lay lul - lay thou ti - ny child

Bye, bye, lul - lay lul - lay._____

PARSLEY, SAGE, ROSEMARY AND THYME — An English Folk Song

Are you go - ing to Scar - bor-ough Fair?

Par - sley, Sage, Rose - mar - y and Thyme. Re -

mem - ber me to one who lives there, For

once she was a true love of mine.

FLATS (♭)

A flat note is played on the next key to the *left* of the 'natural note' with the same letter name — **'B flat'** is played on the black key to the left of **B** and so on.

Flat notes are marked with a flat sign ♭ . (B Flat is written B ♭ .)

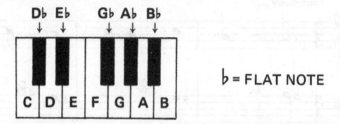

♭ = FLAT NOTE

On the staves, flat notes are shown by a flat sign (♭) in front of the note which is to be 'flattened'. *Play all the notes on the black keys, saying the name of each note as you play it.*

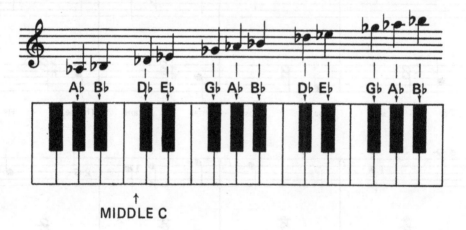

MIDDLE C

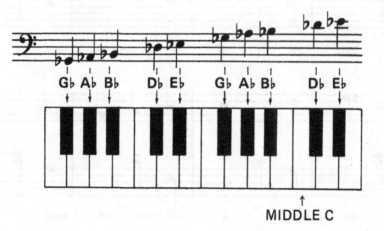

MIDDLE C

Play these examples to practise reading flat notes.

Play this with the left hand.

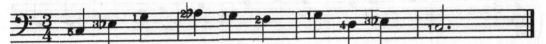

As you will probably have realised by now, the note played on each black key can have either a sharp or flat name.

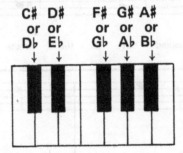

As well as changing the notes marked by them, ♯ and ♭ signs also affect notes in the same position on the stave which follow in the bar—

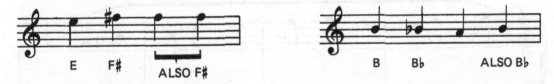

However, if the note is to be sharp or flat in the next bar, the sharp or flat sign will be used again.

NATURAL SIGNS (♮)

A sharp or flat can be cancelled by a 'natural sign' (♮). Written in front of a note, it tells us the natural note is needed instead of a sharp or flat which was marked earlier. This sign also affects all notes in the same position which follow in the bar.

STREETS OF LAREDO — A cowboy song

This tune has sharp and flat notes, which are marked by ♯ or ♭ signs.
The natural signs in brackets — (♮) — are there to remind you that the ♯ or ♭
signs do not affect notes which are in the next bar.

Moderately, with a lilt

(1) (2) 3

As I walked out in the streets of La - re - do, As

I walked out in La - re - do one day I

spied a poor cow - boy all dressed in white lin - en, All

dressed in white lin - en as cold as the clay.

82

WE SHALL OVERCOME — A traditional Spiritual

This tune has some sharp (♯) and flat (♭) notes, along with chords played by the right hand. Follow the fingering carefully so both hands move smoothly and correctly. Look up any notes which you may not remember on page 58, or on pages 77, 80 or 103.

GREENSLEEVES — A old English love song

Read this carefully. The notes marked '(#)' are also **G Sharp** notes because the sharp sign in front of the previous **G** affects all **G** notes which follow in the same bar. The notes marked '(♮)' are plain **G Naturals** because they are in a new bar and do not have sharp signs in front of them.

Continued on next page

Music in different Keys

As you have seen in previous pages, sharps, flats and naturals may be written into music when they are needed to play particular pieces of music. However, sharps and flats are often so much a part of the music that they are shown right at the beginning of each stave, immediately after the clefs. These sharp and flat signs at the beginning of music are called 'Key Signatures' and they tell us which 'key' the music is in.

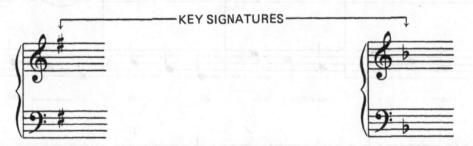

KEY SIGNATURES

Each sharp or flat sign of the key signature is written in the position of a note. It affects ALL NOTES in the music which have the same name as the note marked. Here, the sharp sign is in the position of an 'F' note (shown in brackets). It means EVERY F must be 'sharpened'—

= SHARPEN EVERY F

These are the Sharp Key Signatures which you are most likely to find:

KEYS OF G AND E MINOR

= SHARPEN EVERY F

KEYS OF D AND B MINOR

= SHARPEN EVERY F AND EVERY C

KEYS OF A AND F# MINOR

= SHARPEN EVERY F EVERY C AND EVERY G

KEYS OF E AND C# MINOR

= SHARPEN EVERY F EVERY C EVERY G AND EVERY D

Flat key signatures are similar. Each flat sign is in the position of a note. All notes with the same name must be 'flattened'.

KEYS OF F AND D MINOR	KEYS OF Bb AND G MINOR	KEYS OF Eb AND C MINOR	KEYS OF Ab AND F MINOR
= FLATTEN EVERY B	= FLATTEN EVERY B AND EVERY E	= FLATTEN EVERY B EVERY E AND EVERY A	= FLATTEN EVERY B EVERY E EVERY A AND EVERY D

Different keys enable us to play different combinations of notes to make our music sound more varied and interesting. They also enable us to play higher or lower to suit different singing voices and instruments, when we want to play with them.

Play the scales of the keys of G and F and hear the difference.

In the scale of G, F♯ is played instead of F (natural).

In the scale of F, B♭ is played instead of B (natural).

SCALE OF G (One Sharp)   SCALE OF F (One Flat)

F♯   Bb

The notes of the scale and other notes with the same names, are the melody notes you can expect to find in music in each key.

Extra ♯, ♭ or ♮ signs may be found in music in each key. Remember they also affect notes in the same position which follow in the bar.

Take care to read sharps, flats and naturals correctly, or your music will not sound right. Read these pages again if you have any doubts about sharps, flats, naturals or key signatures.

COCKLES AND MUSSELS — A Folk Song from Ireland

Practise the part each hand plays separately before playing with both hands together. This tune has **B Flat** in the key signature, so play **B♭** instead of **B**, except where the flat is cancelled by a natural sign (♮). (All the flat notes are marked in this tune as a reminder.)

AULD LANG SYNE — An old Scottish melody. Words by Robert Burns
Practise playing separately with each hand before playing with both hands
together. Remember that the key signature with one flat sign means you should
play **B**♭ instead of **B** (natural).

Should auld ac-quain-tance be for-got, and nev - er brought to mind? Should

auld ac-quaint-ance be for-got, and days of auld lang syne? For

auld__ lang__ syne my dear For auld__ lang__ syne. We'll

take a cup of kind - ness yet, For auld__ lang__ syne.

O CHRISTMAS TREE (TANNENBAUM) — A traditional German melody

This tune has one sharp in the key signature, so **F Sharp** should be played instead of **F** — except in the third line where a natural sign (♮) means that **F (Natural)** should be played. Practise the left-hand chords separately before playing with both hands.

O Christmas Tree, O Christmas Tree, Your branches green de - light us. O

Christ-mas Tree, O Christmas Tree, Your bran-ches green de - light us. They're

green when sum - mer days are bright, They're green when win - ter snow is white. O

Christmas Tree, O Christmas Tree, Your branches green de - light us.

90

MINUET IN G — by Johann Sebastian Bach

One sharp in the key signature means **F Sharp** should be played instead of every **F**. Follow the fingering carefully so you play this piece of music smoothly and evenly.

PLAISIR D'AMOUR — by Martini il Tedesco

Here, the right hand plays the melody *and* backing chords. The stems of the melody notes go upwards (♩), those for the backing chords downwards (♪). Make sure each dotted half note (♩.) of the melody is held for a full three beats. *Remember F Sharp is in the key signature.*

Moderately slowly

TUM BALALAIKA — A Yiddish Folk Song

This tune has **B Flat** in the key signature, so flatten every **B**. The notes marked — (**C♯**) — are sharp notes because the ♯ in front of the first **C** also affects the other **C** notes which follow in the same bar.

COPPELIA — by Leo Delibes

Take your time with this piece of music. It is written the key of E♭, with three flats. Remember to play B♭ instead of every **B**, E♭ instead of every **E** and A♭ instead of every **A**, unless they are marked with natural signs (♮).

(1) (2)   3 &   1   2   3 &

How to become a better pianist

By the time you reach this part of the book, you should be on the way to becoming a good pianist — as long as you have learned to play each piece of music correctly before going on to the next. Before you read any further, return to anything you did not understand and read it again. Go back to any music or part of a tune which you found at all difficult, and try it again. The secret of becoming a really good player, is to take the trouble to keep practising each new step until it becomes completely natural.

You are at an important stage. You have learned quite a lot about playing the piano and reading music. Now is the time to polish what you have learned by finding and playing new pieces of music.

From here on, there is some friendly advice to help you to become a better pianist and get even more enjoyment from your playing.

POLISH YOUR PLAYING

Always try to make your music flow smoothly. Make sure each finger strikes the keys with the same force, so that every note sounds as loudly and clearly as the next. Practise using all the fingers of both hands until you can play evenly, smoothly, and naturally, without thinking about what you are doing.

After playing each note, keep your finger in place on the key until you are ready to play the next note — unless a 'rest' is marked in the music. 'Walk' your fingers from one note to the next, so that there are no gaps between notes.

Try playing with your eyes closed sometimes and let your ears tell you whether your fingers are in the right places. This will help you to feel more confident and natural as you play the piano, and make it easier to read music without looking down at your fingers all the time.

If you have a cassette or tape recorder, make a recording of yourself and listen to your playing. Position the microphone to the right of the piano and try different positions until you find the best sound. However, do not put a microphone on the piano as vibrations will spoil the sound.

Listen to your recordings, and you will be able to hear if your playing falters or is uneven. Keep your recordings and mark the date on them. Then, if ever you feel you are not progressing, you can listen to them and hear how much your playing has improved since the recording was made.

PRACTICE

Follow the advice on 'How to practise' given on page 35. Try to learn something new every week, or really polish something you are still learning. Set aside a few minutes every time you play to go over anything which you find at all difficult.

READ MUSIC AS OFTEN AS POSSIBLE

The more you read music, the easier it becomes, so practise reading music whenever you can. Find new music to read — any piano music will do as long as it is not too complicated. Look for books of different types of music in your local library, or buy yourself some music as explained on page 99.

Every new tune will help you to learn to read more quickly and play better. Choose simple music at first — tunes which are not too long, without too many sharps or flats in the key signature.

LEARN FROM OTHER PIANISTS

Listen to piano music as often as you can — on records, and on radio and television. Listen closely to all types of music and different styles of playing, and try to imagine how you would play them.

Go out and watch other people playing, preferably in places where you can get close enough to see what the pianist is doing. The players do not have to be 'big-name performers'. You can learn a lot from anyone who plays in public, as long as you remember the basic rules and do not pick up another musician's bad habits.

Do not be put off by the high standard of playing by musicians you see. Remember they were once beginners, who went through all the steps you are taking.

DO YOU NEED PIANO LESSONS?

If you are happy with what you play, or if you are a 'natural' musician who finds learning very easy, you may manage without taking piano lessons for a while, provided you play enough different music and learn from other players.

However, lessons are essential if you want to play Classical Music or Jazz, or take your piano playing seriously. A good teacher will help you progress far more quickly than you could on your own. He or she will suggest suitable music for you to play, explain how different effects and techniques are played, and help you in many other ways.

If you want to take lessons, choose a teacher who is expert in the music you would like to play. Your music shop or piano dealer may be able to recommend someone and give you an idea of the cost of lessons. Otherwise look for advertisements for piano lessons in local newspapers or music magazines.

Talk to the teacher about your standard of playing and what you would like to learn, before committing yourself to a series of lessons. Also decide whether you would prefer lessons at home or at a teacher's studio or piano school.

Get the most out of your lessons by practising whatever your teacher suggests and strive for a definite improvement between each lesson.

HAVE FUN — PLAY PIANO WITH A FRIEND

You can have a lot of fun playing with a friend who plays another instrument, or accompanying a friend who sings. The extra practice this gives will help your own playing to improve considerably at the same time.

If you do not know anyone who sings or plays another instrument, ask your music shop or a music society, because they may be able to recommend someone. Otherwise, you could advertise on a notice board or in a newspaper.

Do not hesitate to ask people to play music with you. The piano sounds well with most other instruments and you will find many singers and players pleased to have the opportunity to make music accompanied by a piano.

When you play music with someone else, you should choose tunes which you both know well, and read the same music. It is not a good idea to attempt anything new before you have had time to practise it on your own. If you do not know the same tunes, choose a piece of music together and both practise it separately before you play with one another. Always make sure the music is written in the same key for both instruments.

Make sure any other musical instruments are put in tune with the piano before you start to play, or the music will not sound pleasant. This should not be a problem as long as your piano is tuned to 'concert pitch' (see page 13).

Count the beat before you begin, so you both start together at the same speed. To accompany singing, play the first part of the music as an 'Introduction' to give the singer the starting notes.

Learning to play new music

Now you are ready to gain experience by learning to play different pieces of music of your own choice. The easiest way to learn new pieces, is to buy printed music for tunes you like, or borrow it from a library. Look for 'albums' which contain several tunes as they are normally better value than the 'sheet music' for a single tune. Your music shop should have albums of 'easy piano' arrangements in which you will probably find some tunes you would like to play.

Start with short, simple pieces of music, preferably tunes you know well which are not too fast. Avoid music with more than three sharps or flats in the key signature at first, as it will be more difficult to read. When you have learned to play a few 'easy' tunes, you can go on to tunes which are longer, or tunes which are in different keys. Always try to learn something new from each piece of music, and continually strive to improve your playing.

Take each tune in easy stages. Learn one thing at a time — work out what each hand does separately, before you try to play anything complicated with both hands together.

See which sharps or flats are in the key signature, and remember that they affect *every* note with the same name. Work out how you are going to move your fingers smoothly from one note to the next, before you worry about the timing of notes. If any tune does not sound right when you play it, check that you are reading the music correctly and following any sharp, flat or natural signs.

Count out the beat and start playing each tune slowly and evenly, then gradually work up to the correct speed. Practise any awkward parts on their own until you have mastered them. If the timing to part of a tune is not obvious write the counting underneath the notes in pencil. (See pages 62 and 63 if you are unsure about the timing of eighth or sixteenth notes or rests.)

Look for parts of the music which are repeated, as this can save you the trouble of working out everything more than once. (See 'How to read Sheet Music', on the following pages for signs which mean that the music should be played more than once.)

Learn to play every piece of music correctly, before going on to something new, or you may end up knowing how to play parts of several tunes without being able to play any of them completely.

How to read Sheet Music

The music in most albums and sheet music is written for singing or for playing on many different musical instruments, so you need to know which parts are for the piano. The first bars of a typical piece of sheet music normally look something like this, with the melody line shown over the piano part.

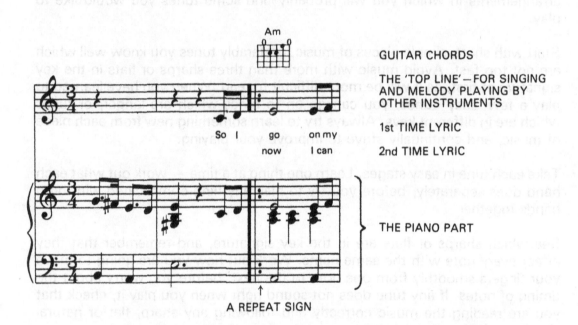

GUITAR CHORDS

THE 'TOP LINE'—FOR SINGING AND MELODY PLAYING BY OTHER INSTRUMENTS

1st TIME LYRIC

2nd TIME LYRIC

THE PIANO PART

A REPEAT SIGN

As you can see here, the 'top line' gives the melody for singing, or playing on other instruments. The part you would normally play on the piano is shown separately underneath.

The piano part also gives the melody in most sheet music, so you can play it as a 'piano solo'. However, occasionally the piano part is an accompaniment or 'backing' which is meant only for playing with another instrument or with a singer.

The backing on its own is not suitable for playing as a piano solo, so check that the melody is included in the piano part before you buy music, if you intend to play the whole tune on the piano. (You can do this by comparing the upper line of the piano part with the 'top line'. *If these two lines appear similar,* the piano music *includes* the melody, even though there may be more notes in the piano part.)

In sheet music, various signs are used if parts of the music are to be played more than once. Make sure you understand how these signs work in each piece of music before you start to play it.

—REPEAT SIGN. This means you should return to a similar sign which is facing the other way — and repeat the music in between.

If there is no other sign, repeat the music from the beginning.

1.
2.
—FIRST and SECOND TIME SIGNS. The first time through, the music includes the part marked — 1.

Second time round, play the music marked — 2.

D.C. —'D.C.' or 'Da Capo' means 'repeat the music from the beginning.'

D.S. —'D.S.' means 'go back and repeat from this sign — %

D.S. %
al Coda ⊕
—This means 'go back to the sign — % — and repeat the music until you come to 'to Coda ⊕'; then go to the music marked 'Coda ⊕'.

The order in which the music is to be played is often obvious in songs from the way the lyrics (words) are written.

In some tunes, the melody is changed slightly for the second or third verses. These changes are often shown with smaller than normal notes.

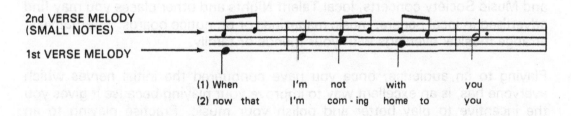

2nd VERSE MELODY
(SMALL NOTES) ⟶

1st VERSE MELODY ⟶

(1) When   I'm   not   with   you
(2) now that   I'm   com - ing   home to   you

How To Read Music, another book by Roger Evans, explains other words, signs, and notes which you may find in music.

Playing to an audience

Sooner or later someone is going to ask you to play the piano for them, or you are going to want to share your music with other people. The same advice applies whether you play for an audience of hundreds, or just your family and friends.

If you are going to play anywhere but in your own home, check the piano to make sure all the keys work properly. Then, make sure the piano sounds in tune. (Do not try to play a piano which is not in good condition because it will spoil your music.) Find a piano stool or seat which is the right height for a good playing position.

Choose music which you know well and which you can play without hesitation. Do not play the most complicated piece you know, or the most recent tune you have learned, as you are more likely to make embarrassing mistakes with these. If you are going to play more than one piece, pick tunes with different rhythms and speeds, in different keys, so your playing does not sound all the same. Mix loud and soft music, and save the best and most dramatic pieces until last.

Work out good beginnings and endings for your tunes to make your playing entertaining and professional-sounding. Try to hear each tune in your head before starting to play to get the speed and the feeling of the music right.

Above all, have confidence in your playing — whatever you play will be enjoyable for your audience as most people like the sound of the piano.

Never announce that 'you cannot play very well', or 'you will probably make mistakes' — this kind of talk is likely to make you do these very things. If you do make a mistake, make a joke of it or ignore it — most people will probably not notice a mistake anyway. *Never* play with cold hands, because your fingers will be stiff.

There are many places where you can play in public if you want to — College and Music Society concerts, local Talent Nights and other places you may find advertised in local papers, music magazines or on notice boards. Alternatively, arrange musical evenings with your friends or family.

Playing to an audience, once you have conquered the initial nerves which everyone has, is an excellent way to improve your playing because it gives you the incentive to play better and polish your music. Practise playing to an audience by looking out of a window while you play and imagining that the whole world is watching and listening to you, or play to a cassette or tape recorder.

Note Directory

Use this page to look up any notes which you may not remember.

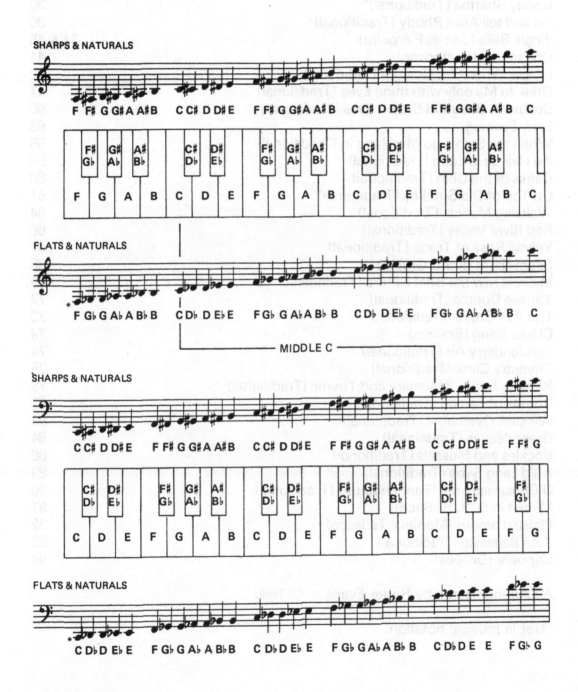

SHARPS & NATURALS

FLATS & NATURALS

MIDDLE C

SHARPS & NATURALS

FLATS & NATURALS

*Read these lines from right to left

MUSIC IN THIS BOOK Page

All Arrangements by Roger Evans   © 1980

*Not in musical notation.